Loyalty and

Those Who HONOUR YOU

DAG HEWARD-MILLS

Parchment House

Unless otherwise stated, all Scripture quotations are taken from the
King James Version of the Bible.

THOSE WHO HONOUR YOU

Copyright © 2016 Dag Heward-Mills

First published 2019 by Parchment House
1st Printing 2019

Find out more about Dag Heward-Mills at:

Healing Jesus Campaign
Write to: evangelist@daghewardmills.org
Website: www.daghewardmills.org
Facebook: Dag Heward-Mills
Twitter: @EvangelistDag

ISBN : 978-1-64329-194-9

Contents

Contents

CHAPTER 1

Honour Relationships

RENDER therefore to all their dues: tribute to whom tribute is due; custom to whom custom; fear to whom fear; HONOUR TO WHOM HONOUR.

Romans 13:7

Giving honour is a biblical command. You are expected to give honour to whom honour is due. Not everyone is due honour! However, some people are due honour and must be given their due honour! *If you do not give honour to whom honour is due, you will never have the right relationship with certain people.* Great relationships flourish when honour is given where it is due. No honour, No great relationships!

Honour is important in all relationships. But honour is *critical* in certain relationships. Honour is not that important in your relationship with friends, cousins, acquaintances and schoolmates. However, honour is *very important* in your relationship with God the Father, the Son and the Holy Spirit, your prophet, your pastor, your husband and other such authority figures.

1. **Honour the Father and it will give life to your relationship with your heavenly Father.**

    Wherefore the Lord God of Israel saith, I said indeed that thy house, and the house of thy father, should walk before me for ever: but now the Lord saith, Be it far from me; for THEM THAT HONOUR ME I WILL HONOUR, and they that despise me shall be lightly esteemed.

    1 Samuel 2:30

Honour is an important thing for every Christian to know about. Honour is very important in your relationship with God. God is the creator of heaven and earth and He expects to be honoured. If you honour Him, He will honour you. God does not take dishonour lightly. Dishonouring God is a dangerous thing.

Some people honour their relatives more than they honour God! Some people honour their children more than they honour God! Some people honour their wives more than they honour God! God looks at the honour you give to others in relation to the honour that you give to Him. He wants to be the most honoured and most valued person in your life! If you honour and value anyone more than you honour and value Him, He will react to it and you will not like the reaction. You can ask Eli what happened to him when he honoured his children and his family more than he honoured God.

Today, Christians are honouring family more than they honour God. They do things to please wives and children more than to please God. Because of this, the mission field and the harvest fields lack certain quality labourers. All the quality educated and intelligent labourers, work for the United Nations, work for the banks, work for the businesses and work for the governments of this world. The work of God suffers and has many poorly educated people with low IQs, trying to do their very best for Jesus. This is because men honour the United Nations, the banks, the businesses and the governments of our world more than they honour God. People are prepared to travel and sacrifice and give up their home countries for the sake of the United Nations, the World Health Organisation, the businesses and the banks of the world. I know a country in West Africa that has at least five thousand of its young men in the British army. These young men and their families are happy to be sent to dangerous war zones like Afghanistan, Kosovo, Somalia, Yemen, etc. Over the years, I have noticed how the citizens of this same West African country find it impossible to go on Christian missions to plant churches in countries that are known to be much safer.

Eli discovered the hard way that God would not stand to be honoured less than his family. He experienced one of the most withering curses of all time for honouring his sons above God. This is why I am writing this all-important book about honour.

You will either be someone who honours God or someone who dishonours God. Which one will you be?

2. **Honour Jesus and it will give life to your relationship with Him.**

   He that receiveth you receiveth me, and he that receiveth me receiveth him that sent me.

                                                        Matthew 10:40

Honouring Jesus is very important. Jesus is very concerned about how you treat him. If you honour Jesus, you will be blessed greatly. How do you honour Jesus Christ? The Bible teaches us how we can honour Jesus Christ.

a. If you honour a man who is sent by Jesus, you are honouring Jesus. If you despise a man sent by Jesus, you are despising Jesus who sent him.

He that heareth you heareth me; and he that despiseth you despiseth me; and he that despiseth me despiseth him that sent me.

Luke 10:16

b. If you honour Christians, you are honouring Jesus. Whatever you do to the least of the brethren you are doing it to Jesus Himself.

And the King shall answer and say unto them, Verily I say unto you, INASMUCH AS YE HAVE DONE IT UNTO ONE OF THE LEAST OF THESE MY BRETHREN, YE HAVE DONE IT UNTO ME.

Matthew 25:40

Saul was shocked to find out this stunning reality on the road to Damascus. Whatever honour you give to the least of the brethren, you are giving it to Jesus. Whatever despisement, persecution or dishonour you give to the least of His brethren, you are giving it to Jesus. When Saul was persecuting the church, Jesus took it personally and reacted against Saul. He said, "I am Jesus whom you are persecuting." Be careful how you treat the brethren. Honour Jesus by honouring the brethren!

c. If you honour Jews, you are honouring Jesus. Whatever you do to the least of the brethren you are doing it to Jesus Himself. Israel, the Jews, are the brethren of Jesus. Remember that Jesus is the most famous Jew that ever lived. It is important to honour the nation of Israel. As we honour Jews, we are honouring the brethren of Jesus.

And as he journeyed, he came near Damascus: and suddenly there shined round about him a light from heaven: And he fell to the earth, and heard a voice saying unto him, Saul, Saul, why persecutest thou me? And he said, Who art thou, Lord? And the Lord said, I am Jesus whom thou persecutest: it is hard for thee to kick against the pricks.

Acts 9:3-5

3. **Honour the Holy Spirit and it will give life to your relationship with Him.**

Of how much sorer punishment, suppose ye, shall he be thought worthy, who hath trodden under foot the Son of God, and hath counted the blood of the covenant, wherewith he was sanctified, an unholy thing, and hath done DESPITE UNTO THE SPIRIT OF GRACE?

Hebrews 10:29

Notice the word "despite"! You must be careful not to dishonour the Holy Spirit in any way. Trifling with the anointing and people that are anointed can be dangerous. When you dishonour the Holy Spirit, you are worthy of sore punishment. Learn to give honour to the Holy Spirit.

Those who do not respect the Spirit live to regret it. The Holy Spirit requires great respect. Never make the mistake of doing despite unto the Spirit of grace.

Learn to honour the anointing! Learn to honour the Holy Spirit! Those who honour the Holy Spirit develop a deep relationship with the Holy Spirit. King David honoured the Holy Spirit many times and in many ways. That is why he was so anointed and that is why his kingship was so different from the others. Honour truly gives life to relationships!

David gave life to his relationship with the Holy Spirit when he honoured the presence of the Holy Spirit on Saul, his enemy. Saul was hunting for David's life! Saul was trying to kill him.

But because of the Holy Spirit's anointing on Saul, he would not fight back. David would not attack anything that had been anointed. He had great reverence for the anointing. No wonder King David's relationship with the Holy Spirit flourished.

Seven Times David Refused to Attack Someone Who Was Anointed

Saying, Touch not mine anointed, and do my prophets no harm.

Psalms 105:15

And he said unto his men, The Lord forbid that I should do this thing unto my master, the Lord's anointed, to stretch forth mine hand against him, seeing he is the anointed of the Lord.

1 Samuel 24:6

Behold, this day thine eyes have seen how that the Lord had delivered thee to day into mine hand in the cave: and some bade me kill thee: but mine eye spared thee; and I said, I will not put forth mine hand against my lord; for he is the Lord's anointed.

1 Samuel 24:10

And David said to Abishai, Destroy him not: for who can stretch forth his hand against the Lord's anointed, and be guiltless?

1 Samuel 26:9

The Lord forbid that I should stretch forth mine hand against the Lord's anointed: but, I pray thee, take thou now the spear that is at his bolster, and the cruse of water, and let us go.

1 Samuel 26:11

This thing is not good that thou hast done. As the Lord liveth, ye are worthy to die, because ye have not kept your master, the Lord's anointed. And now see where the king's spear is, and the cruse of water that was at his bolster.

1 Samuel 26:16

The Lord render to every man his righteousness and his faithfulness: for the Lord delivered thee into my hand to day, but I would not stretch forth mine hand against the Lord's anointed.

1 Samuel 26:23

When King David died, he was remembered as the sweet and anointed psalmist of Israel. Instead of being remembered for his sins, he is remembered for the anointing. Instead of being remembered as a political and governmental leader, he is remembered as an anointed psalmist. If you honour the Holy Spirit, the Holy Spirit will honour you.

Now these be the last words of David. David the son of Jesse said, and the man who was raised up on high, THE ANOINTED of the God of Jacob, and the SWEET PSALMIST of Israel, …

2 Samuel 23:1

4. Honour your prophet and it will give life to your relationship with your prophet.

But Jesus said unto them, a prophet is not without honour, but in his own country, and among his own kin, and in his own house. And HE COULD THERE DO NO MIGHTY WORK, save that he laid his hands upon a few sick folk, and healed them.

Mark 6:4-5

When prophets are honoured, the anointing upon them comes alive. Jesus, a mighty prophet, could not do mighty works simply because he was not honoured by the people of Nazareth. There are many people who are sent into your life as prophets. Prophets that are honoured do mighty works! Great prophets do minor works when they are not honoured.

You must be careful how you handle prophets. Mishandling them can lead to barrenness and desolation in your life. Jesus was unable to minister His miracle power to people who needed it because they simply did not honour Him.

Most of the people I prophesied to, did not know that I was prophesying to them. They found out years later that I was actually prophesying to them. Most of these people related with me as a friend, a senior brother, a concerned Christian, or at best, an over-zealous pastor. Because they did not honour me as a prophet, I kept prophesying to them and they kept on missing the message.

Indeed, I have prophesied to many people who did not honour me. They did not receive me as a prophet and they did not honour me, so God did not open their eyes so they could see and believe. People who were destined to be rich became poor because they did not receive the power of God and the message from a prophet. I have watched as people who were destined to work with me lost their places because they did not believe when I was speaking to them as a prophet. Their failure to honour me as a prophet destroyed their relationship with me. Honour your prophet and it will give life to your relationship with your prophet!

5. **Honour "fathers" and it will give life to your relationship with fathers.**

    HONOUR THY FATHER and mother; (which is the first commandment with promise;) That it may be well with thee, and THOU MAYEST LIVE LONG on the earth.

    Ephesians 6:2-3

The person who teaches you and feeds you may become a father to you. Many people stand in the place of a father when they minister to you. Honouring them is important because they are truly fathers to you. Giving honour to a father invokes the promise of a good and long life.

6. **Honour your pastor and it will give life to your relationship with your pastor.**

Let the elders that rule well be counted worthy of double honour, ESPECIALLY THEY WHO LABOUR IN THE WORD AND DOCTRINE.

1 Timothy 5:17

It is easy to ignore what a pastor does for you! The other day, I saw pictures of a congregation wailing and mourning at their pastor's funeral. What an outpouring of love, deep sorrow and anguish it was! I wonder if the pastor knew how honoured he was when he was alive! You must honour your pastor because he watches over your soul.

Obey them that have the rule over you, and submit yourselves: for they watch for your souls, as they that must give account, that they may do it with joy, and not with grief: for that is unprofitable for you.

Hebrews 13:17

The pastor is someone who has been sent into your life to watch over you and shepherd you to eternity. You must honour those who are sent to you. If you honour someone who is sent to you, you are honouring the Father.

Do not do anything that is outside the Bible. But if it is in the Bible, you must follow it so that you will have the blessings. Showing honour is one of the most important spiritual exercises you can engage in. Instead of doing nothing, do something and remember these rules for honouring servants of God.

That all men should honour the son, even as they honour the Father. HE THAT HONOURETH NOT THE SON HONOURETH NOT THE FATHER WHICH HATH SENT HIM.

John 5:23

Honour belongs to and is bestowed on anyone who is sent to you. When you bestow honour on the servant you honour the sender. That is why ambassadors are honoured carefully; because they represent entire powerful nations. Jesus represented Almighty God. Jesus represented heaven. To dishonour Jesus was the greatest mistake the Jews could ever make.

Let the elders that rule well be counted worthy of DOUBLE HONOUR, especially they who labour in the word and doctrine.

1 Timothy 5: 17

You must honour your pastor because he is worth double to you. You must honour your pastor in the way the Bible prescribes. Double honour is extra honour that is given to someone who deserves it. Double honour is to reward a person with twice as much as he should have received, for his inputs. To dishonour someone is to fail to reward him or to pay him adequately for his great contribution, inputs and his worth to your life.

The scriptures teach us that pastors who rule well must be honoured. Those who rule are those who lead you and those who pastor you. We can see from the Word that they are worthy of honour. That means it is appropriate and fitting that they be honoured. When you do not honour pastors, your relationship with them will not flourish.

Honour is important to prevent ingratitude and forgetfulness. God does not like people who forget things that have been done for them. Ingratitude kills relationships! God Himself is not unrighteous to forget your good works. When you are ungrateful and forgetful about what your pastor has done for you, you place yourself in spiritual danger. No church member is neutral.

Whoso rewardeth evil for good, evil shall not depart from his house

Proverbs 17:13

7. Honour your husband and it will give life to your marriage relationship.

When Vashti did not give honour to her husband the king, the relationship with her husband came to an end. Indeed, there are certain relationships that require respect and honour. Honour gives life to the marriage relationship. Once the level of honour drops, the quality of marriage life correspondingly falls.

For this deed of the queen shall come abroad unto all women, so that THEY SHALL DESPISE THEIR HUSBANDS IN THEIR EYES, when it shall be reported, The king Ahasuerus commanded Vashti the queen to be brought in before him, but she came not.

Esther 1:17

CHAPTER 2

The Rewards of Honour

Now a certain man was sick, named Lazarus, of Bethany, the town of Mary and her sister Martha. (It was that Mary which anointed the Lord with ointment, and wiped his feet with her hair, whose brother Lazarus was sick.) Therefore his sisters sent unto him, saying, Lord, behold, he whom thou lovest is sick. When Jesus heard that, he said, this sickness is not unto death, but for the glory of God, that the Son of God might be glorified thereby.

John 11:1-4

Mary and Martha are the ultimate examples of those who reap the benefits of honour. Mary and Martha honoured Jesus and they reaped all the rewards of honour. Remember, it was Mary who anointed the Lord's feet and wiped his feet with her hair. The honour they bestowed on Jesus was unparalleled! We sing about it today and remember these two individuals.

Mary and Martha reaped the rewards of honour. Notice: Mary had Jesus sitting in her house! Mary had her dead brother raised! Mary and Martha had ultimate miracles! Mary and Martha were close to Jesus! Mary and Martha had access to Jesus Christ! Mary and Martha are in heaven today! Mary and Martha are memorialized! Mary and Martha are more popular than some of the apostles! Mary and Martha are more known than many of the disciples of Jesus! And it is all because of the honour they bestowed on Jesus!

1. Those who honour experience supernatural power.

Those who honour receive supernatural power! Honour is rewarded with mighty works from the one you honour. Jesus could not do mighty works when he was with people who did not honour Him. Mighty works of miracles and healing are denied those who do not honour. There are needs everywhere. I remember a young lady who honoured me with a little offering. When I prayed with her over her offering, I saw someone who could be her husband. A few minutes after she honoured me with her little offering, God gave her a miracle husband. Indeed, it is a miracle to have a husband! There are countries that have ten million more women than men. In other words, there are ten million women who cannot and will not find husbands in their country.

2. Those who honour receive great miracles.

People who show honour can expect great miracles! Jesus did not go where people had needs, but to where He was honoured! There are problems everywhere. But Jesus went to the house of Lazarus and Mary where He had been received, loved and honoured. Mary and Martha loved Jesus Christ! They cared for him personally and ministered to him directly.

3. Those who honour will have personal access

Then Martha, as soon as she heard that Jesus was coming, went and met him: but Mary sat still in the house.

John 11:20

It is not easy to get close to great people. Imagine how difficult it will be in your lifetime to meet a president. Indeed, it can be very difficult to meet a great man of God. Mary and Martha had access to Jesus Christ. Mary and Martha could send messages to Jesus and He would receive them. They sent Him a message that their brother was not well. Mary and Martha had access to Jesus Christ. Martha walked to Jesus and spoke to Him directly. Mary and Martha had access to Jesus when he was eating. Mary could actually sit at the feet of Jesus.

Now it came to pass, as they went, that he entered into a certain village: and a certain woman named Martha received him into her house. And she had a sister called Mary, which also sat at Jesus' feet, and heard his word.

Luke 10:38-39

4. Those who honour will experience close and intimate fellowship.

Now it came to pass, as they went, that he entered into a certain village: and a certain woman named Martha received him into her house. And she had a sister called Mary, which also sat at Jesus' feet, and heard his word.

But Martha was cumbered about much serving, and came to him, and said, Lord, dost thou not care that my sister hath left me to serve alone? Bid her therefore that she help me.

And Jesus answered and said unto her, Martha, Martha, thou art careful and troubled about many

things: But one thing is needful: and Mary hath chosen that good part, which shall not be taken away from her.

Luke 10:38-42

Mary and Martha were close and intimate with Jesus. He would solve personal quarrels that they had. Jesus ate food cooked by Martha! Most important people do not eat just anything. Jesus relaxed in Mary and Martha's home and he relaxed in their company! Most important people are not relaxed everywhere. Most important people do not relax in your company. The Bible actually shows that Jesus relaxed in the home of Mary and Martha.

Martha and Mary hosted Jesus Christ in their home. They are known for feeding him and looking after him personally. It is no wonder that Jesus chose them for mighty miracles. The mightiest miracle ever heard of among men was done personally for Mary and Martha. Indeed, mighty miracles are done for those who bestow honour on God's servants.

5. Those who honour will experience extra love.

Now Jesus loved Martha, and her sister, and Lazarus.

John 11:5

God so loved the world that He gave His only begotten son. Apart from Jesus loving the whole world and dying for the whole world, Jesus is mentioned as specifically loving Martha, her sister Mary and Lazarus. I do not know of any other human being whom Jesus is said to have loved like this. Please remember which Mary it was. It was that Mary who anointed the Lord with ointment, and wiped his feet with her hair, whose brother Lazarus was sick.

6. Those who honour will receive more honour.

Verily I say unto you, wheresoever this gospel shall be preached throughout the whole world, this also that

she hath done shall be spoken of for a MEMORIAL of her.

Mark 14:9

Honour is rewarded with more honour. When you sow honour you reap honour!

You reap what you sow. This lady is known throughout the world. Many of the disciples of Jesus are not known.

Most people would struggle to mention the names of the twelve disciples. This lady reaped the honour she bestowed on Jesus a million times more! She honoured Jesus Christ in a little home in a little village in Israel but she has been honoured throughout the whole world. She is mentioned millions of times because of what is recorded about her in the most published book in the world. She could not have known that the honour she was bestowing on Jesus would go that far.

Do you sometimes wonder why you are not honoured in this life? Do you wonder why no one honours you? It is probably because you do not honour anyone yourself.

How will you ever be honoured when you are a man who never honours another? Why would anyone want to honour you! How come you never make reference to your father, your pastor or any other man of God? You do not seem to have anybody above you. You never give honour to anyone. Do not ever expect to be honoured. Honour begets honour!

7. Those who honour will receive divine protection.

And Jesus said, LET HER ALONE; why trouble ye her? She hath wrought a good work on me.

Mark 14:6

Those who honour receive divine protection. Jesus defended Mary when everyone attacked her. She was criticised by the people around. She was viewed with suspicion. Her motives were questioned. "Why is she getting close to Jesus? What does she really want from Him?"

But Jesus defended Mary! Jesus protected Mary and Jesus forgave her sins! People you honour always look kindly on you! Your boss is likely to overlook your mistakes when he senses the admiration and honour that you have for him! The person you honour always looks kindly on you!

CHAPTER 3

Levels of Honour

RENDER therefore to all their dues: tribute to whom tribute is due; custom to whom custom; fear to whom fear; HONOUR TO WHOM HONOUR.

Romans 13:7

A re there levels of honour? Are there higher ways and lower ways in which you can be honoured?

In this chapter, I will show you how to recognize how much you are being honoured as a pastor or leader. There are greater and greater levels of honour you can receive. What does this mean? It means, you can be honoured from one level to another. Let us look at these different levels of honour.

1. The first level of honour is when you are recognized.

And he went out from thence, and came into his own country; and his disciples follow him. And when the sabbath day was come, he began to teach in the synagogue: and many hearing him were astonished, saying, From whence hath this man these things? And what wisdom is this which is given unto him, that even such mighty works are wrought by his hands?

IS NOT THIS THE CARPENTER, the son of Mary, the brother of James, and Joses, and of Juda, and Simon? And are not his sisters here with us? And they were offended at him. But Jesus said unto them, a prophet is not without honour, but in his own country, and among his own kin, and in his own house. And he could there do no mighty work, save that he laid his hands upon a few sick folk, and healed them.

Mark 6:1-5

Why is being recognized important? If people do not recognize who you are they often do not honour you. If they do not honour you, they do not believe in you. When they do not believe in you, your ministry does not work among them. When Jesus Christ came to Jerusalem, He was not recognized as the Messiah. They did not honour Him. Instead, they killed Him and shortened His life.

They recognized Jesus as a carpenter. They recognized Jesus as the son of Mary. They recognized Jesus as one of five brothers. They recognized Jesus as the brother of James, Joses, Juda and Simon.

How could this man whom they knew as a carpenter be the Son of God? Because they failed to recognize Him as the Son of God, they failed to honour Him!

When God sends men amongst us, it is very important that we recognize them. It is also very important how quickly we recognize them. When you fail to recognize a good person, he will move on to where he is recognized. It is not good to stay amongst people who do not acknowledge you.

The ability of people to acknowledge you is key to their ability to honour you.

As a man of God, you may or may not be recognized for who you are. I realise that some of the greatest pastors are not recognized by their fellow ministers. In fact, they are actually despised by those who live with them in the same city. Some of the greatest prophets are not acknowledged or even noticed in their own countries. Most people recognize what is loud and colourful. It may not even be noteworthy but shallow men often honour insignificant and unsubstantial things that do not deserve honour.

When you are not acknowledged, always remember that you are not being honoured. When you are not acknowledged, you are not being taken seriously. Move on to the places where you are honoured.

On the road to Emmaus, the disciples walked along with Jesus and listened to His questions and answers. They called Him a stranger because they did not recognize who He was. They related to Him as a completely different person from whom He really was.

And, behold, two of them went that same day to a village called Emmaus, which was from Jerusalem about threescore furlongs. And they talked together of all these things which had happened. And it came to pass, that, while they communed together and reasoned, Jesus himself drew near, and went with them. But their eyes were holden that they should not know him. And he said unto them, what manner of communications are these that ye have one to another, as ye walk, and are sad? And the one of them, whose name was Cleopas, answering said unto him, ART THOU ONLY A STRANGER in Jerusalem, and hast not known the things which are come to pass there in these days?

Luke 24:13-18

I was once in a foreign country where I was being honoured by the church there. There was a visiting minister from my own country who just happened to be passing by. When he saw the honour that was bestowed on me, he remarked, "It is sad that he is not recognized for who he is in his own country."

2. The second level of honour is when they listen to you gladly.

And when Jesus saw that he answered discreetly, he said unto him, Thou art not far from the kingdom of God. And no man after that durst ask him any question. And Jesus answered and said, while he taught in the temple, How say the scribes that Christ is the Son of David? For David himself said by the Holy Ghost, The Lord said to my Lord, Sit thou on my right hand, till I make thine enemies thy footstool. David therefore himself calleth him Lord; and whence is he then his son? AND THE COMMON PEOPLE HEARD HIM GLADLY.

Mark 12:34-37

The common people in Israel honoured Jesus. How do we know that? We know that He was honoured by these people because they listened to him gladly. *When you pay attention to what someone is saying you are honouring the person.* If a person is excited to hear from you, he has a lot of respect for you. Those who do not respect you may listen to you but not gladly. Your enemies and mockers may be forced to listen to you, but they do not listen gladly. *Those who love you and honour you will listen to you gladly.*

21

Some years ago, I had to choose a church to pastor and develop. I prayed about it. I decided to go where I was honoured. How would I know who honoured me? As I thought about it, I realised that students were the ones who heard me gladly. They loved my preaching and they loved to wait around just to hear me say a few words.

There were others who looked sleepy and tired when I preached to them. There were those who looked harassed when I called for a meeting. But the students looked excited to be called for every meeting. Indeed, it was not difficult for me to know where I had the greatest honour. Where the people heard me gladly was where I was being honoured.

3. The third level of honour is when they change their behaviour.

But if ye be without chastisement, whereof all are partakers, then are ye bastards, and not sons. Furthermore we have had FATHERS OF OUR FLESH WHICH CORRECTED US, AND WE GAVE THEM REVERENCE: shall we not much rather be in subjection unto the Father of spirits, and live?

Hebrews 12:8-9

Obedience and a change of lifestyle is a great sign of respect. When you change your behaviour and begin to do something differently just because someone told you so, it is a sign that you respect the person greatly. Sometimes when a married couple are having intractable problems that they cannot resolve, a more senior and respected person is brought in to see if his words will make a difference. Because the couple respects the senior person, they listen and change their ways.

Respect and honour are always a reason for change. Sometimes, the instruction does not make sense but honour and respect will make people obey.

For years, I advised people against taking loans and getting into debt. Most of the people I spoke to did not respect me.

They simply went right ahead and took all the loans they felt they should take. Apart from them having their own opinion about debt (which I respect) there is an element of disregard when someone totally ignores all you say.

Every preacher has people who do not respect him. A lot of people do not respect Jesus Christ. What Jesus has taught us about eternity does not matter to them. You will be judged for what you dishonour!

God asked the children of Israel to keep His Sabbaths as a sign of respect to Him. God saw the keeping of the Sabbath as respect. He said, "Keep my Sabbaths and reverence me." *Whenever you change your behaviour, change your life, change something you do, you show your respect to the one who spoke to you.* Failure to obey is failure to honour!

Ye shall KEEP MY SABBATHS, AND REVERENCE my sanctuary: I am the Lord.

Leviticus 19:30

4. *The fourth level of honour is when they receive your agents, your messengers and your delegated servants.*

Then began he to speak to the people this parable; A certain man planted a vineyard, and let it forth to husbandmen, and went into a far country for a long time. And at the season he sent a servant to the husbandmen, that they should give him of the fruit of the vineyard: but the husbandmen beat him, and sent him away empty.
And again he sent another servant: and they beat him also, and entreated him shamefully, and sent him away empty.
And again he sent a third: and they wounded him also, and cast him out. Then said the lord of the vineyard, what shall I do? I WILL SEND MY BELOVED SON: IT MAY BE THEY WILL REVERENCE HIM WHEN THEY SEE HIM.
But when the husbandmen saw him, they reasoned among themselves, saying, this is the heir: come, let us kill him, that the inheritance may be ours. So they cast him out of

23

the vineyard, and killed him. What therefore shall the lord of the vineyard do unto them? He shall come and destroy these husbandmen, and shall give the vineyard to others. And when they heard it, they said, God forbid.

Luke 20:9-16

The next stage of honour is to respect people that are sent to you. *Respect for someone is shown by the respect you show to his servant whom he sends to you.* In the story above, you will see that the Lord of the vineyard expected some reverence to be shown to his emissaries. He said, "It may be that they will reverence him when they see him."

Over the years, I have noticed that people who respect the people whom I work with are showing me respect. When they reverence the person I have sent, they reverence me. When they reject the people that I work with, they are rejecting me.

The regard for the person I work with and I have sent, is the honour they give me. It is the honour they express for my decisions and my judgments. It is nice for them to smile sheepishly and speak softly to the important person. It is nice for them to claim that they love and respect you. It is nice for them to present offerings in the name of honour. But we can see through their hypocrisy by the way they relate to the servants that are sent to them. Jesus said, "He who receives you receives me."

Many people simply do not understand that they will have to accept servants who are sent to them.

5. The fifth level of honour is when they honour you when you are not present.

When the even was come, there came a rich man of Arimathaea, named Joseph, who also himself was Jesus' disciple: HE WENT TO PILATE, AND BEGGED THE BODY OF JESUS. Then Pilate commanded the body to be delivered. And when Joseph had taken the body, HE WRAPPED IT IN A CLEAN LINEN CLOTH, AND LAID IT IN HIS OWN NEW TOMB, which he had hewn out in the rock: and he rolled a great stone to the door of the sepulchre, and departed. And there was Mary Magdalene, and the other Mary, sitting over against the sepulchre.

Matthew 27:57-61

The next stage of honour is to honour someone when he cannot see you nor hear you honouring him. Joseph of Arimathea honoured Jesus when he was dead. Jesus could not hear him negotiating with Pilate to take his body. Jesus was not there to see Joseph of Arimathea begging for His body from Pontius Pilate.

Jesus could not see Joseph of Arimathea wrapping His body in a white linen cloth. Jesus could not hear the loving words and acts of Joseph of Arimathea. Jesus did not see how Joseph of Arimathea donated his new expensive tomb to Him. It was an offering that was done in secret.

Most people give honour when it can be seen! They want you to know that they are saying nice words and doing nice things. Why is that? When someone gives honour, he expects to be rewarded for his good deeds of showing honour. He expects to be seen of men and receive payback one day. When you honour someone who cannot see what you are doing, there is no way he can pay you back. It is because of our deep hypocrisy that we love to show respect in a way that can be paid back.

I was once preaching at a camp meeting and made mention of a man of God. I had often mentioned this man of God in my preaching but this time it was different because his son was sitting in the meeting. I felt uneasy after the service. So I called the son and said to him, "Do not think that I am mentioning your father's name because you are sitting here. For many years, I have mentioned his name in my camp meetings. I have given him honour many times, even though he is not present." You see, I wanted to make the point that I was not giving honour to his father because he was present.

There is a higher and more genuine level of giving honour when you do so without being seen or acknowledged by men.

6. *The sixth level of honour is when people give you sacrificial gifts.*

A son honoureth his father, and a servant his master: IF THEN I BE A FATHER, WHERE IS MINE HONOUR? and if I be a master, where is my fear? saith the Lord of hosts unto you, O priests, that despise my name. And ye say, wherein have we despised thy name? Ye offer polluted bread upon mine altar; and ye say, wherein have we polluted thee? In that ye say, the table of the Lord is contemptible. And if ye offer the blind for sacrifice, is it not evil? AND IF YE OFFER THE LAME AND SICK, IS IT NOT EVIL? OFFER IT NOW UNTO THY GOVERNOR; will he be pleased with thee, or accept thy person? saith the Lord of hosts.

Malachi 1:6-8

The next level of honour is to present sacrifices and gifts to a person. As you can see, there are many ways to show honour long before you present a sacrifice or gift. *There are people who never present sacrifices or gifts.* There are many reasons for this.

Five Reasons Why People Do Not Give Gifts or Sacrifices

a. Sometimes people are too busy to present gifts, which also means they are too busy to honour you.

b. Sometimes people expect to receive gifts but never give gifts to anyone. This means they expect to receive honour but do not give honour to anyone.

c. *Sometimes people are self-absorbed and indifferent to the greatness of another.* This means they are self-absorbed and indifferent to the honour that is due others.

d. Sometimes people do not respect you or honour you because they have not been taught the word of God.

e. *Sometimes people feel that they do not have disposable income so they cannot present a sacrifice or a gift.* Once again, disposable income speaks of rubbish that you throw away; something you can dispose of.

These are common reasons why they do not present any gift or sacrifice. However, the Bible is clear about honouring with substance. As the prophet said, "If I am a father, where is mine honour?" Indeed, if you really honour someone, there will be a time when you will have to present a sacrifice or a gift to the person.

One day, Kenneth Hagin received a whole suitcase of clothes from his church members. When he opened it, it was the used and discarded clothes of the congregation. As they went through the items, it was clear that most of the clothes were so worn out that they could not be used. He asked his wife to throw the suitcase of clothes out. He said to his wife, "if it is not good for them it is not good for us."

Honouring someone is not about throwing your waste on the person. It is not about giving your disposable income. It is about honour! A sacrifice will always cost you something. Let's be serious!

7. *The seventh level of honour is when they honour you for eternity.*

For ye have the poor with you always, and whensoever ye will ye may do them good: but me ye have not always. She hath done what she could: she is come aforehand to anoint my body to the burying. Verily I say unto you, WHERESOEVER THIS GOSPEL SHALL BE PREACHED THROUGHOUT THE WHOLE WORLD, THIS ALSO THAT SHE HATH DONE SHALL BE SPOKEN OF FOR A MEMORIAL OF HER.

Mark 14:7-9

The seventh stage of honour is the honour that only God can give. Most people are forgotten soon after they die. Only a few

27

people are remembered after they die. Indeed, the memory of most people is erased forever within a few years of their death. Jesus promised this lady that she would be remembered forever. It has happened practically. Today, I am writing about her and reminding everybody of the honour she showed Jesus Christ. This woman is better known than most of the disciples.

As you serve God, you must seek the honour that comes from above. How long will your church or your ministry last? How long will the effect of your ministry remain upon the earth? Is what you are doing a temporary thing? God wants you to bear fruit that will last. Pray that God will touch your fruit so that it will last forever. Without those words spoken by Jesus, this woman would soon have been forgotten.

Think about Matthew, Mark, Luke and John. Each of them wrote a short pamphlet about Jesus Christ. They have been honoured because they wrote about Jesus Christ. They are the four top bestselling authors in the world today. Today, the pamphlets they wrote to honour Jesus have spread all over the world. They are the most printed and reprinted books in the whole world.

Who would have thought that the works of Matthew, Mark, Luke and John would survive hundreds of years of history? It is only when God touches your work that your memory remains forever. Pray for the honour that comes from above and you will be honoured forever. No man can honour you in this eternal way.

CHAPTER 4

How to Honour Someone by Thinking Properly

And when the sabbath day was come, he began to teach in the synagogue: and many hearing him were astonished, saying, FROM WHENCE HATH THIS MAN THESE THINGS? AND WHAT WISDOM IS THIS WHICH IS GIVEN UNTO HIM, THAT EVEN SUCH MIGHTY WORKS ARE WROUGHT BY HIS HANDS? IS NOT THIS THE CARPENTER, THE SON OF MARY, THE BROTHER OF JAMES, AND JOSES, AND OF JUDA, AND SIMON? AND ARE NOT HIS SISTERS HERE WITH US? AND THEY WERE OFFENDED AT HIM. But Jesus said unto them, a prophet is not without honour, but in his own country, and among his own kin, and in his own house. And he could there do no mighty work, save that he laid his hands upon a few sick folk, and healed them.

Mark 6:2-5

You can show honour without giving something physical to the person. This type of honour is what I call honouring *"without"* substance.

Jesus marvelled about how He was not honoured. *What did His lack of honour consist of? It consisted of the people questioning Him, not believing in Him, doubting Him and being offended at Him.* Jesus was not complaining that people were not giving him offerings! Jesus was speaking about a different kind of honour.

It is at this point that Jesus said, *"A prophet is without honour in his own country."* At that material moment, Jesus was being dishonoured by the people who were listening to him preach. The people failed to believe in Him without questioning His background, His sincerity, His integrity and His calling. That was the dishonour that Jesus Christ noted on that fateful day.

When I started out in the ministry, I was questioned rigorously and relentlessly by the people who listened to me. "Who called you? How do you know you are called? Are you a real pastor? Do you have the gifts of God? Are you not a medical student? Are you not just twenty-five years old? Are you not proud to call yourself a pastor? Who ordained you? Who appointed you? Who do you think you are? You cannot even preach well! Are you sure God is pleased with you? Are you not an imposter? Are you not proud?" These are the questions that those who had no honour for me asked.

Some people think that honour is just about giving money to someone. You must learn about the honour that can be ministered to a person without necessarily giving something physical. This is the honour that is not by giving money. Let us look at several ways you can honour someone without necessarily giving him substance.

It is important to know what honour actually is.

To honour someone is to think well of him, to hail him or to praise him. Questioning a person, suspecting a person, distrusting a person, doubting his words and disbelieving his prophecies mean you do not honour him.

A son therefore honours his father when he praises his father. When a son dishonours his father, he accuses him, he blames him, he denounces him, he reproaches him, he disgraces him, he humiliates him and he rejects him.

And when they were escaped, then they knew that the island was called Melita. And the barbarous people shewed us no little kindness: for they kindled a fire, and received us every one, because of the present rain, and because of the cold. And when Paul had gathered a bundle of sticks, and laid them on the fire, there came a viper out of the heat, and fastened on his hand.

And WHEN THE BARBARIANS SAW THE VENOMOUS BEAST HANG ON HIS HAND, THEY SAID AMONG THEMSELVES, NO DOUBT THIS MAN IS A MURDERER, WHOM, THOUGH HE HATH ESCAPED THE SEA, YET VENGEANCE SUFFERETH NOT TO LIVE. And he shook off the beast into the fire, and felt no harm.

Howbeit they looked when he should have swollen, or fallen down dead suddenly: but after they had looked a great while, and saw no harm come to him, THEY CHANGED THEIR MINDS, AND SAID THAT HE WAS A GOD. In the same quarters were possessions of the chief man of the island, whose name was Publius; who received us, and lodged us three days courteously.

And it came to pass, that the father of Publius lay sick of a fever and of a bloody flux: to whom Paul entered in, and prayed, and laid his hands on him, and healed him. So when this was done, others also, which had diseases in the island, came, and were healed: WHO ALSO HONOURED US WITH MANY HONOURS; and when we departed, they laded us with such things as were necessary.

Acts 28:1-10

31

To dishonour someone is to accuse, to blame, to denounce, to reproach, to disgrace, to humiliate, to disrespect and to condemn someone. The apostle Paul was initially denounced, disrespected and condemned as a murderer on the island of Malta.

Initially, the people thought that Paul was a murderer. They suspected he was a very evil man with a terrible history of gruesome murders in his background. Such evil thoughts about a person will not make you honour him. Such thoughts are dishonourable. It is because people have negative thoughts about you that the power of God does not work. Negative thoughts are a clear sign of the absence of honour.

However, when Paul did not die from the snakebite, they changed their minds. They thought highly of him. They even thought that he could be a god. Now, when Paul laid hands on Publius' father, a miracle occurred and Publius' father was healed. Many sick people on the island were brought to Paul and were also healed. Then, the good thoughts about Paul abounded. Many people saw him as a good person. They thought of him as a man of God. *They thought of Paul as a man sent from God!* They did not question his background any more. From then on, the people of Malta honoured Paul. Up till today, in the twenty-first century, Apostle Paul is honoured on the island of Malta.

Perhaps, the members of your church do not honour you and that is why your ministry does not flourish. Members of a church need to honour their pastor so that the power of God on his life will be activated. "Honour" has a lot to do with the way you think about a person.

CHAPTER 5

How to Honour Someone by Acknowledging Him

Thou shalt rise up before the hoary head, and honour the face of the old man, and fear thy God: I am the Lord.

Leviticus 19:32

To honour someone is to notice him! To honour someone is to give him attention because he is worthy of it. Therefore to dishonour someone is to disregard, ignore and to neglect the person.

This is why we mention people's names at programmes and acknowledge their presence. It is to say that we have noticed that they came for the programme. Sometimes, when special mention is not made of a dignitary who made the effort to attend, he feels dishonoured. You did not notice his presence!

But Jehoshaphat said, is there not here a prophet of the Lord, that we may enquire of the Lord by him? And one of the king of Israel's servants answered and said, here is Elisha the son of Shaphat, which poured water on the hands of Elijah.

And Jehoshaphat said, the word of the Lord is with him. So the king of Israel and Jehoshaphat and the king of Edom went down to him. And Elisha said unto the king of Israel, What have I to do with thee? get thee to the prophets of thy father, and to the prophets of thy mother.

And the king of Israel said unto him, Nay: for the Lord hath called these three kings together, to deliver them into the hand of Moab.

AND ELISHA SAID, AS THE LORD OF HOSTS LIVETH, BEFORE WHOM I STAND, SURELY, WERE IT NOT THAT I REGARD THE PRESENCE OF JEHOSHAPHAT THE KING OF JUDAH, I WOULD NOT LOOK TOWARD THEE, NOR SEE THEE. But now bring me a minstrel. And it came to pass, when the minstrel played, that the hand of the Lord came upon him.

2 Kings 3:11-15

When Elisha met the rebellious king of Israel, he pointed out that he would not have even looked towards him because he did not respect him. Failing to lift up your head to look at someone is a sign of your lack of respect for him. Indeed, the word "disregard" means to "not regard" or "not see".

34

Elisha pointed out to the king of Israel that even if he had looked in his direction he would not have seen him. Watch out for those who do not notice your presence! It is the first stage of dishonour. Watch out for those who refuse to notice your presence or existence!

When you are noticed it is because you are being honoured. When you are disregarded or ignored, it is because you are not being honoured. Jesus said, "A prophet is not without honour except in his own country." In other words, a prophet may be ignored in his own country. He may not be noticed nor regarded in his own country.

To dishonour someone is therefore to fail to notice and remember a person, his achievements and his worth. Leaving a person to self-announce and self-promote his own worthiness is leaving a person to honour himself. It is a sure sign that he is not honoured.

When a person walks into his home and all heads are fixed on their phones, he feels unnoticed. When people do not even lift up their heads from their phones to say "hello" or "welcome" the person has been disregarded, dishonoured and unnoticed. Couples who walk around silently in the house without noticing each other any more have stopped honouring each other's presence.

How to Acknowledge Someone

1. **Honour someone by making public mention of the person.** When you mention a person's name in a speech or a sermon, you honour the person.

2. **Honour someone by publicly acknowledging his presence.** Mentioning that a person is present at a meeting is a way of recognizing someone. Recognizing your presence at a meeting is a form of recognition and therefore a form of honour.

3. **Honour someone by giving an award.** Being given an award is a sign that you are recognized. Awards are a form of recognition. If awards are given to others, but not to you, in spite of your great achievements then you are being dishonoured. Your achievements are not recognized. Those who are being given the awards are those who are being acknowledged.

4. **Honour someone by inviting him to be a speaker.** Being invited to speak is a sign of recognition. When you are asked to speak at a programme, it is a sign of recognition.

5. **Honour someone by appointing him to an honourable position.** Being appointed to a board or to a position is a sign that you are being recognized.

How to Know That You Are Not Honoured

1. When you are never mentioned it is a sign that you are not recognized.

2. When public acknowledgment of your presence is not made, you are not recognized.

3. When you are not given awards in spite of your obvious achievements in an area, it is a sign that you are not recognized.

4. When you are never invited to be a speaker, it is a sign that your ministry is not recognized.

5. When you are not appointed to be on a board or given any important job, it is a sign that you are not recognized.

CHAPTER 6

How to Honour Someone by Adapting to Him

Then Pharaoh sent and called Joseph, and they brought him hastily out of the dungeon: and HE SHAVED HIMSELF, AND CHANGED HIS RAIMENT, and came in unto Pharaoh.

Genesis 41:9-14

The adaptation of someone to you is the proof that he honours you. To honour someone is to accommodate him, to adjust to him and to adapt to the person. Therefore, your accommodating someone, your adjusting to someone and your adapting to someone are manifestations of your honour for the person. Similarly, your failure to adapt, to adjust and to accommodate someone are clear manifestations of a lack of honour. There are several people in the Bible who adapted themselves to others. Their adaptation was a sign of their honouring that person. Let's go through the list of people in the Bible who adapted themselves as a sign that they honoured a person.

1. Ruth adapted and adjusted herself to Boaz.

Then Naomi her mother in law said unto her, My daughter, shall I not seek rest for thee, that it may be well with thee? And now is not Boaz of our kindred, with whose maidens thou wast? Behold, he winnoweth barley to night in the threshingfloor. WASH THYSELF THEREFORE, AND ANOINT THEE, AND PUT THY RAIMENT UPON THEE, and get thee down to the floor: but make not thyself known unto the man, until he shall have done eating and drinking. And it shall be, when he lieth down, that thou shalt mark the place where he shall lie, and thou shalt go in, and uncover his feet, and lay thee down; and he will tell thee what thou shalt do.

Ruth 3:1-4

Ruth adjusted and adapted herself to the man Boaz by washing herself, anointing herself and putting on appropriate clothes. Indeed, when a woman is in awe of her husband, she will carefully present herself to him. She will wash, she will clean and she will put on the best clothes and the best perfumes so that she is all that a man wants from a woman.

When the woman no longer has the same awe and honour that she had at the beginning, she will no longer wash, clean or anoint herself. She will no longer concern herself with what she wears at home. Many women wear rags at home. They basically wear stained or torn clothes that cannot be worn in public. The Bible teaches that a wife should give honour to her husband as the head.

> And when the king's decree which he shall make shall be published throughout all his empire, (for it is great,) ALL THE WIVES SHALL GIVE TO THEIR HUSBANDS HONOUR, both to great and small.
>
> Esther 1:20

The woman who does not adapt herself to her husband is dishonouring him. A newly-married woman who is seeking to honour her new husband will adjust many things in order to please him. She will adjust the time that she comes home. She will adjust the company that she keeps. She will adjust her eating habits. She will adjust the food that she eats. She will adjust the television programmes that she watches. She will adjust the clothes that she wears. She will adjust the time that she sleeps. She will adjust the time that she wakes up. She may even adjust the time that she goes to the toilet, to make room for him. Indeed, when the love and the honour are gone, all these adjustments and adaptations will stop.

2. Esther adapted herself to her new husband.

> Now when every maid's turn was come to go in to king Ahasuerus, after that she had been twelve months, according to the manner of the women, (for so were the days of their purifications accomplished, to wit, SIX MONTHS WITH OIL OF MYRRH, AND SIX MONTHS WITH SWEET ODOURS, AND WITH OTHER THINGS FOR THE PURIFYING OF THE WOMEN;) Then thus came every maiden unto the king; whatsoever she desired was given her to go with her out of the house of the women unto the king's house.
>
> Esther 2:12-13

You will adapt yourself to the person you honour. Esther had honour for the king she was about to meet so she soaked herself in oil and perfumes for twelve months. Women who honour their husbands will prepare for them and will adjust their lives to suit their husbands'.

A certain husband was being counselled about his failure to have sex with his relatively new bride. For a long time he refused to explain why he was unable to approach his wife.

Finally, he explained that his wife's hidden parts were indeed in need of grooming. He described scenes of swampy, marshy, overgrown and unkempt undergrowth. He said he was simply unable to navigate his way through what he felt was an unpleasant, uninviting and sometimes, repulsive environment. Indeed, his wife was a pretty girl who had many different hair styles for the general public. Obviously, she was more conscious of adapting herself to the general public and to outsiders. Whatever her husband saw or experienced was not so important to her.

As you can see, this lady did not know that she needed to adjust and adapt to her husband. Adjusting and adapting yourself is a sign that you honour someone. Coming as you are is not a sign of honour. Adjusting is a sign of honour!

3. Vashti did not adjust herself to her husband, the king.

On the seventh day, when the heart of the king was merry with wine, he commanded Mehuman, Biztha, Harbona, Bigtha, and Abagtha, Zethar, and Carcas, the seven chamberlains that served in the presence of Ahasuerus the king, To bring Vashti the queen before the king with the crown royal, to shew the people and the princes her beauty: for she was fair to look on. But the queen Vashti refused to come at the king's commandment by his chamberlains: therefore was the king very wroth, and his anger burned in him.

Esther 1:10-12

Vashti was an older wife who was tired of adjusting herself and adapting to her husband. She was saying to herself, "This nonsense must stop! How long will I be asked to do such silly things?" She simply refused to adjust her life and obey her husband.

The whole realm of King Ahasuerus was outraged at the refusal of the king's wife to adapt herself to her husband's desires. Indeed, many wives grow tired of the adjustments that they have to make. They are tired of the adjustments they have to make to please the whims and fancies of the man.

One lady whose husband had died was asked whether she would marry again. She simply answered, "Never again. I cannot give myself to this silly "open and close" business any more. You see, this lady had been married for many years and had been opening up and closing up for her husband to enjoy himself for many years. She was no longer willing to adjust her life to something that she did not really want or enjoy.

4. Joseph adjusted himself to the Pharaoh.

Then spake the chief butler unto Pharaoh, saying, I do remember my faults this day: Pharaoh was wroth with his servants, and put me in ward in the captain of the guard's house, both me and the chief baker: And we dreamed a dream in one night, I and he; we dreamed each man according to the interpretation of his dream. And there was there with us a young man, an Hebrew, servant to the captain of the guard; and we told him, and he interpreted to us our dreams; to each man according to his dream he did interpret. And it came to pass, as he interpreted to us, so it was; me he restored unto mine office, and him he hanged.

> Then Pharaoh sent and called Joseph, and they brought him hastily out of the dungeon: and HE SHAVED HIMSELF, AND CHANGED HIS RAIMENT, and came in unto Pharaoh
>
> Genesis 41:9-14

When you work for someone you respect and honour, you will adjust yourself to be able to work with him. When Joseph was called upon by Pharaoh, he decided to improve his presentation and make himself look good. He shaved because not everyone likes bearded faces. He decided to change his old prison clothes so that his appearance would be pleasing to the king. Perhaps Joseph was used to certain types of clothes and a certain way of keeping his hair. *His adjustment was a sign of the honour that he had for Pharaoh.*

When you work for someone, it is important that you adjust yourself to the person. If you realise that the person you work for has certain preferences, your respect for the job and for the person will cause you to adapt. Just as Joseph shaved in honour of Pharaoh, a spouse who honours her husband may have to shave certain parts if it pleases her husband.

If the person you work for does not use Facebook or WhatsApp as a way of communicating, you will adapt yourself and find the appropriate technology that will enable you to communicate with him. All that is a sign of your adaptation and your respect. If your mother or your father is unable to use WhatsApp, you cannot say that you cannot communicate with them any more. You, the child, have to adapt yourself to whatever technology the grown-up is comfortable with.

Pride will not allow you to adapt and adjust yourself to the person you must honour. When a person refuses to communicate because he called a number of times but got no answer, it is usually pride at work. The person that you honour will never be too difficult to make contact with.

I once gave a man a job to make some windows. It was a big contract and his job was to manufacture windows and install them in a large church building. As the project went on, I needed to meet with this contractor from time to time. The only time I could meet this contractor was on Sundays because, that was when I was in the church, and that was the best time for me to inspect the project. Unfortunately, this contractor was very irritated about being called on Sundays or having to come to the church on a Sunday afternoon. I am sure you know the end of this story. The contract came to an end abruptly. That contractor was too "big" to work for me.

I have had many workers, masons, carpenters, plumbers, electricians and contractors who have worked for me for thirty years. All those who have successfully worked for me have adjusted and adapted themselves to my times and seasons. I have even had workers who worked for me on Christmas day. They considered it an honour to be asked to do anything for me at Christmas time. They considered it an honour to do something small for the one who had helped them to have a job every day for the past twenty-five years. They had never been without a contract for the last twenty-five years. The least you can do, when you want to honour someone, is to adapt yourself, adjust yourself and accommodate the person you honour.

I watched a documentary on a lady who had worked for a Prime Minister of England. She worked for him successfully for many years till he died. She described how he liked dictating notes when he was sitting on the toilet. Perhaps this lady had to adapt to this unusual style of taking down notes. She would obviously have to adapt to the smell or noises coming from the toilet and make no disrespectful or embarrassing comment about it. It could be that his leadership ideas flourished most when he was on the toilet! Adapt yourself, adjust yourself and show real honour to the one you claim to respect!

5. Daniel, Hananiah, Mishael and Azariah had to "adjust" their choice of food in order to work with the king.

Children in whom was no blemish, but well favoured, and skilful in all wisdom, and cunning in knowledge, and understanding science, and such as had ability in them to stand in the king's palace, and whom they might teach the learning and the tongue of the Chaldeans.

And the king appointed them a daily provision of the king's meat, and of the wine which he drank: SO NOURISHING THEM THREE YEARS, THAT AT THE END THEREOF THEY MIGHT STAND BEFORE THE KING.

Now among these were of the children of Judah, Daniel,
Hananiah, Mishael, and Azariah:

Daniel 1:4-6

You will adapt yourself to the person you honour. Daniel
and his team knew that they would have to adjust their diet just
because they were going to be with the king. They had to adjust
and adapt to what happened in the palace so that they could be
with the king. There are people who don't want to adjust to
the food of the king when they are called to the king's palace.
Adaptation of your culinary tastes is an important adaptation for
someone you honour.

Some people were brought up never drinking tea. Some
people have never drunk coffee. Some people have never eaten
potatoes. Some people are only used to eating local food from
the village. You may have to adjust yourself to the person you
honour and learn how to drink tea or coffee. Many English people
drink tea, not to satisfy their hunger, but as a social drink. Failing
to drink tea at the right time may be deemed anti social or may
even be a sign of you dishonouring the occasion.

Some years ago, I was honoured to sit by a great man of God
for a special dinner in Korea. It was one of the greatest honours
of my lifetime. It was a special Korean dinner. As the food was
served, I was taken aback because I was not used to most of
the dishes. But this was a great occasion and I was sitting by a
famous man of God who had honoured me by asking me to sit by
him. I pulled myself together quickly and ate up everything that
was before me. It is indeed a sign of honour to adapt yourself to
the food that is being presented by the one that you honour.

6. Daniel, Hananiah, Mishael and Azariah had to "adjust" their names in order to work with the king.

Children in whom was no blemish, but well favoured,
and skilful in all wisdom, and cunning in knowledge, and
understanding science, and such as had ability in them to stand
in the king's palace, and whom they might teach the learning and
the tongue of the Chaldeans.

And the king appointed them a daily provision of the king's meat, and of the wine which he drank: so nourishing them three years, that at the end thereof they might stand before the king.

Now among these were of the children of Judah, Daniel, Hananiah, Mishael, and Azariah: UNTO WHOM THE PRINCE OF THE EUNUCHS GAVE NAMES: FOR HE GAVE UNTO DANIEL THE NAME OF BELTESHAZZAR; AND TO HANANIAH, OF SHADRACH; AND TO MISHAEL, OF MESHACH; AND TO AZARIAH, OF ABEDNEGO.

Daniel 1:4–7

Even your name may have to be adjusted if you want to successfully work with the king. The ability to adapt to your new name is a sign of your honour. For whatever reason, the king seemed not to be able to pronounce the names of the Jewish eunuchs. He gave them his own names. As you can see he was totally bending them to be fully adjusted to him. It is a great privilege when you receive a name from the king. You would greatly dishonour the king if you despised or rejected the name.

I have given names to different people and have had different responses. Some were so happy to be given a name, that they changed their names in their passports, and in all official documents. Some even went to court to swear upon various documents that their names were changed. They were so honoured and so happy to have received a new name. All their friends and relatives were told about their new name. They did not allow anyone to refer to them by their old name. I noticed their responses and I felt that I had the honour of a father who had given a name to his child.

However not everyone had the same response to the names I gave. I did not receive the same honour from everyone whose name I changed. I once gave a name to someone and this person dishonoured me by despising the name time and time again, until I virtually regretted giving the name. This person never used the name outside my circles. All the family members and old friends still used the old name. It was almost as though the new name was a bother. Indeed the person never changed the name or added it to any official document. It was as though the name was used in my presence just to humour me. Shadrach, Meshach and Abednego were names given to them by King Nebuchadnezzar. They accepted these names and lived with them as though they were their birth names. Today, we mention the names Shadrach, Meshach and Abednego as though they are Jewish names. They are in actual fact the Babylonian names given to the Jewish eunuchs. They deemed it an honour to be given a name by the one they worked for.

CHAPTER 7

How to Honour Someone by Paying Attention to His Words

My son, ATTEND TO MY WORDS; incline thine ear unto my sayings.

Proverbs 4:20

Hearken unto me now therefore, O ye children, and ATTEND TO THE WORDS of my mouth.

Proverbs 7:24

1. Honour your father by paying attention to his words.

Children, OBEY your parents in the Lord: for this is right. HONOUR thy father and mother; (which is the first commandment with promise;) That it may be well with thee, and thou mayest live long on the earth.

Ephesians 6:1-3

Paying attention to your parents' words is very important. Obeying your parents is the same as honouring your parents. You dishonour me when you are disobedient. Obeying your parents is the honour that you can give to them. The scripture is clear on the fact that you must honour your parents. In the same breath, the scripture teaches that we should obey our parents.

Your addiction to a person's words reveals the honour you have for the person. Your addiction to the words of Jesus reveal the honour you have for Jesus. Your addiction to a person's messages reveals the honour and respect you have for his words. Those who do not listen to the preaching messages are the ones who do not respect the message.

Paying attention to someone's words or advice is the evidence that you honour him. Whom you listen to, whom you follow and whose words you attend to is a sign of the person you really honour.

I once advised a brother to play golf for his health and for a host of other good reasons. However, he did not take my advice seriously and never played golf. One day however, I met this brother playing golf and I was amazed that he had taken up this sport that he had had so many reasons not to engage in. At a later discussion I found out that he had been reading a book by Lee Kuan Yew. Lee Kuan Yew was the famous founder of Singapore and was a golfer. This brother was apparently more impressed with the advice from Lee Kuan Yew than from myself about the need to play golf. He was much more willing to comply with the advice coming from Lee Kuan Yew than from me.

I noticed how he paid more attention to the words of Lee Kuan Yew than to my words. The one you pay attention to is the one you honour. Whose words do you pay attention to? Whose advice do you pay attention to?

2. Honour your father by paying attention without answering back or arguing.

Exhort servants to BE OBEDIENT unto their own masters, and to please them well in all things; NOT ANSWERING AGAIN;

Titus 2:9

Servants are asked to obey and pay attention to their instructions. Paying attention causes you not to answer back. Continuous retorts and arguments in defence of your action are a sign of a lack of respect and a lack of honour.

When you are listening to instructions you do not answer back. It takes time to form an answer. This is the reason why people who argue a lot never change their minds.

3. Honour someone by paying attention to all instructions, big or small.

His mother saith unto the servants, WHATSOEVER HE SAITH UNTO YOU, DO IT. And there were set there six waterpots of stone, after the manner of the purifying of the Jews, containing two or three firkins apiece. Jesus saith unto them, fill the waterpots with water. And they filled them up to the brim. And he saith unto them, Draw out now, and bear unto the governor of the feast. And they bare it.

John 2:5-8

Jesus' mother warned the waiters to obey all the instructions given by Jesus.

Most people do not obey all the instructions.

Your deference, your yielding, your agreeing and your compliance with all instructions are manifestations of your honour for someone. Many people obey what they think is sensible and leave out what they think is not necessary.

By leaving out certain instructions, you are saying that some of the instructions given were nonsense! You despise those instructions! You have no respect for those inappropriate instructions. You have no respect for those domestic instructions.

By your actions, you declare that you utterly reject all nonsensical, inapplicable instructions that are given. Seething with indignation and pride, you utterly ignore useless instructions that are given to you.

Dear friend, one of the greatest points of honour is paying attention to all instructions, especially the little things.

CHAPTER 8

How to Honour Someone With Your Substance

HONOUR the Lord WITH THY SUBSTANCE, and with the firstfruits of all thine increase:

Proverbs 3:9

There are two types of honour described in the Bible. There are also two types of honour described in the dictionary. You can honour someone with substance and you can also honour him without substance. "Honour the Lord with your substance!" This is a famous saying from the book of Proverbs. This scripture is teaching you to honour someone by giving something tangible.

Jesus taught us that we will never be free from the need to honour our fathers and mothers with substance. Notice the scripture below:

> He went on, "Well, good for you. You get rid of God's command so you won't be inconvenienced in following the religious fashions! Moses said, 'Respect your father and mother,' and, 'Anyone denouncing father or mother should be killed.' But you weasel out of that by saying that it's perfectly acceptable to say to father or mother, 'Gift! What I owed you I've given as a gift to God,' thus relieving yourselves of obligation to father or mother. You scratch out God's Word and scrawl a whim in its place. You do a lot of things like this."
>
> Mark 7:9-13 (MSG)

1. Honour with your substance by presenting something the person does not need and cannot use.

> For every beast of the forest is mine, and the cattle upon a thousand hills.
> I know all the fowls of the mountains: and the wild beasts of the field are mine. IF I WERE HUNGRY, I WOULD NOT TELL THEE: FOR THE WORLD IS MINE, and the fulness thereof.
>
> Psalms 50:10-12

The gift you give represents the person's worth and greatness to you. Your gift may not be something the person can ever use. Most great people cannot use the gifts you give them. There are gifts you present only for the sake of honour.

One day a man called me up and gave me two new cars. He said, "I have watched your ministry from afar and I feel I should encourage you and honour you. I know you will not drive these cars but I am giving them anyway to honour you." Indeed, he was right. I could not drive those cars because I already had a car that I was using. But I had people that needed them and I immediately passed on the cars to them. What a blessing for them who sowed those seeds! It was not a seed given to meet my needs. It was a seed to honour me.

Many times, to honour someone is to present something valuable that he doesn't need. Your gift is presented for the sake of "honour" only.

His achievements, his worth or his very existence in your life are honoured by your presentation.

Obviously God does not eat the first fruits of the dollars you present to him. You present gifts to God to honour him, not because he is hungry. God does not eat beef or pork. God does not eat biscuits. God does not use United States dollars in heaven. God does not need any of the things we present to Him. They are just our honour for God.

2. Honour with your substance by presenting something physical, substantial and <u>usable</u>.

A son honoureth his father, and a servant his master: if then I be a father, where is mine honour? And if I be a master, where is my fear? saith the Lord of hosts unto you, O priests, that despise my name. And ye say, wherein have we despised thy name?

Ye offer polluted bread upon mine altar; and ye say, wherein have we polluted thee? In that ye say, the table of the Lord is contemptible.

And if ye offer the blind for sacrifice, is it not evil? and if ye offer the lame and sick, is it not evil? Offer it now unto thy governor; will he be pleased with thee, or accept thy person? saith the Lord of hosts.

Malachi 1:6-8

Honour with your substance by presenting a usable gift to a person. Many gifts are unusable. Many people have vases, crystal bowls and unused crockery in their homes. Sometimes, they have wedding presents that have never been opened or used. Most of these presents are in faded cardboard boxes. People love to present these unusable items as gifts. Special chocolate that no one in their houses can eat, is presented to you as an exotic gift. What you must realise is that what is unusable to you is also unusable to me! Notice the scripture above. The prophet warns about presenting blind and lame animals which are no longer useful to the Lord. If you don't want these animals as part of your flock, why do you present them as a gift on the altar? What you cannot use in your house, God cannot use!

3. Honour with substance by following what was done for Mordecai.

On that night could not the king sleep, and he commanded to bring the book of records of the chronicles; and they were read before the king. And it was found written, that Mordecai had told of Bigthana and Teresh, two of the king's chamberlains, the keepers of the door, who sought to lay hand on the king Ahasuerus. And the king said, What honour and dignity hath been done to Mordecai for this? Then said the king's servants that ministered unto him, There is nothing done for him.

And the king said, Who is in the court? Now Haman was come into the outward court of the king's house, to speak unto the king to hang Mordecai on the gallows that he had prepared for him. And the king's servants said unto him, Behold, Haman standeth in the court. And the king said, Let him come in. So Haman came in. And the king said unto him, WHAT SHALL BE DONE UNTO THE MAN WHOM THE KING DELIGHTETH TO HONOUR? Now Haman thought in his heart, To whom would the king delight to do honour more than to myself?

And Haman answered the king, For the man whom the king delighteth to honour, LET THE ROYAL APPAREL

BE BROUGHT WHICH THE KING USETH TO WEAR, AND THE HORSE THAT THE KING RIDETH UPON, AND THE CROWN ROYAL WHICH IS SET UPON HIS HEAD: AND LET THIS APPAREL AND HORSE BE DELIVERED TO THE HAND OF ONE OF THE KING'S MOST NOBLE PRINCES, THAT THEY MAY ARRAY THE MAN WITHAL WHOM THE KING DELIGHTETH TO HONOUR, AND BRING HIM ON HORSEBACK THROUGH THE STREET OF THE CITY, AND PROCLAIM BEFORE HIM, THUS SHALL IT BE DONE TO THE MAN WHOM THE KING DELIGHTETH TO HONOUR.

Then the king said to Haman, Make haste, and take the apparel and the horse, as thou hast said, and do even so to Mordecai the Jew, that sitteth at the king's gate: let nothing fail of all that thou hast spoken.

Esther 6:1-10

The king asked a crucial question. *What should be done to the man whom the king wants to honour?* Haman thought to himself that the king would want to honour him. So he gave a rundown of what should be done to a person who was going to be honoured. Please note the elements of this great honour. Royal clothing! A special horse (a form of transportation)! A crown! Public acclamation and recognition!

The greatest example of uninhibited honouring with substance is seen in the honouring of Mordecai by the king. This scripture answers all the questions about what to do when you want to honour someone.

4. Honour with substance by doing something expensive for the person you want to honour.

And being in Bethany in the house of Simon the leper, as he sat at meat, there came a woman having an alabaster box of ointment of spikenard very precious; and she brake the box, and poured it on his head. And there were some that had indignation within themselves, and said, Why was this waste of the ointment made? For IT MIGHT HAVE BEEN SOLD FOR MORE THAN THREE HUNDRED PENCE, and have been given to the poor. And they murmured against her.

Mark 14:3-5

Do something costly and expensive for the person you honour! There are times you must set aside all restraints and shower the person you wish to honour with something expensive.

Many people wait for the person to die before they show unbridled, uninhibited love and honour. Funerals that spare no expense are held for people who cannot see what is happening. When they were alive, there were all sorts of reasons for not spending money. It is too expensive! It is too extravagant! It is not necessary! It is not our style! When they are dead, people want to buy the most expensive coffin and pay five hundred thousand dollars to buy a lot for their burial in a special garden cemetery.

Jesus memorialised this lady because she honoured him without restraint and without concern for what people thought. She honoured him in time and she spared no expense. To some, it was a waste, but to God it was not a waste of money!

5. **Honour with substance by giving a good honorarium to the prophet who has blessed you. Your honorarium is evidence of your honour.**

Then said Saul to his servant, But, behold, if we go, what shall we bring the man? for the bread is spent in our vessels, and there is not a present to bring to the man of God: what have we?

And the servant answered Saul again, and said, Behold, I have here at hand the fourth part of a shekel of silver: that will I give to the man of God, to tell us our way.

1 Samuel 9:7-8

The expense made on you is a sign of honour. I once visited a church where I ministered powerfully for a number of days and invested heavily in the church. I invested in the church by stabilising their leaders and instilling a sense of honour and respect for their pastor. Later that year, another man of God from a certain nation was invited to preach in the same church.

This man of God gave conditions for his coming. He had to have a number of first class tickets to fly from his country to this African nation. Also he had to be paid a large sum of money for preaching (Some people charge thousands of dollars a day for their ministry. They consider it to be a "brand" which they must not allow to be cheapened.) I was amazed that this church was happy to pay these sums of money because they seemed to have run out of money when I was ministering there.

Indeed, they did not reward me for my ministry with anything like what they did for this other man of God. Obviously, they regarded and honoured the input of this international speaker much more than they regarded and honoured me.

You see, the expenses made on you, the rewards, the honorarium, the salaries, the bonuses you receive are all indications of the honour shown to you and your ministry. When expensive gifts and items are bestowed on a prophet, it is a sign of honour on his life. Where there is no substantial reward, no substantial gift, no substantial honorarium, it is a sign that you are not honoured. Many ministers are not honoured in their own churches.

6. Honour with substance by rewarding the person who has been a blessing to you.

All through the Bible, God's servants are honoured with substance because they are a blessing to the people. Never think to yourself that it is not a biblical practice to honour God's servant. It is your ignorance that makes you feel that honouring God's servant is wrong. Notice these few examples of honour presented to Apostles, Prophets and even angels.

a. Paul was honoured after he was a blessing to the island of Malta.

And when they were escaped, then they knew that the island was called Melita. And the barbarous people shewed us no little kindness: for they kindled a fire, and received us every one, because of the present rain, and because of the cold. And when Paul had gathered a bundle of sticks, and laid them on the fire, there came a viper out of the heat, and fastened on his hand.

And when the barbarians saw the venomous beast hang on his hand, they said among themselves, No doubt this man is a murderer, whom, though he hath escaped the sea, yet vengeance suffereth not to live. And he shook off the beast into the fire, and felt no harm. Howbeit they looked when he should have swollen, or fallen down dead suddenly: but after they had looked a great while, and saw no harm come to him, they changed their minds, and said that he was a god. In the same quarters were possessions of the chief man of the island, whose name was Publius; who received us, and lodged us three days courteously.

And it came to pass, that the father of Publius lay sick of a fever and of a bloody flux: to whom Paul entered in, and prayed, and laid his hands on him, and healed him. So when this was done, others also, which had diseases in the island, came, and were healed: WHO ALSO HONOURED US WITH MANY HONOURS; and when we departed, they laded us with such things as were necessary

Acts 28:1-10

b. Balak wanted to honour Balaam for his prophecies

And Balak sent yet again princes, more, and more honourable than they. And they came to Balaam, and said to him, Thus saith Balak the son of Zippor, Let nothing, I pray thee, hinder thee from coming unto me: For I will promote thee unto very GREAT HONOUR, and I will do whatsoever thou sayest unto me: come therefore, I pray thee, curse me this people.

Numbers 22:15-17

c. Manoah, the father of Samson, wanted to honour the angel who brought him good news of the birth of Samson.

And Manoah said unto the angel of the Lord, What is thy name, that when thy sayings come to pass WE MAY DO THEE HONOUR?

Judges 13:17

CHAPTER 9

Signs of Dishonour

He is despised and rejected of men; a man of sorrows, and acquainted with grief: and we hid as it were our faces from him; HE WAS DESPISED, AND WE ESTEEMED HIM NOT.

Isaiah 53:3

1. Your absence can be a sign of dishonour

And Samuel said unto him, The Lord hath rent the kingdom of Israel from thee this day, and hath given it to a neighbour of thine, that is better than thou. And also the Strength of Israel will not lie nor repent: for he is not a man, that he should repent.

THEN HE SAID, I HAVE SINNED: YET HONOUR ME NOW, I PRAY THEE, BEFORE THE ELDERS OF MY PEOPLE, AND BEFORE ISRAEL, AND TURN AGAIN WITH ME, THAT I MAY WORSHIP THE LORD THY GOD.

1 Samuel 15:28-30

The presence of someone at your event is evidence that you have been honoured. When Saul realised he had lost his position, he begged Samuel to be present at the church service. Samuel's presence would be a sign of respect for Saul. Your presence at certain functions is a sign of your respect for the person. Your presence at someone's wedding is a sign that you respect them. Indeed, your absence at important functions may be deemed as a sign of dishonour.

2. Your failure to call on someone can be a sign of dishonour

And when they were come into the house, they saw the young child with Mary his mother, and fell down, and worshipped him: and when they had opened their treasures, they presented unto him gifts; gold, and frankincense, and myrrh. And being warned of God in a dream that they should not return to Herod, they departed into their own country another way.

THEN HEROD, WHEN HE SAW THAT HE WAS MOCKED OF THE WISE MEN, was exceeding wroth, and sent forth, and slew all the children that were in Bethlehem, and in all the coasts thereof, from two years old and under, according to the time which he had diligently enquired of the wise men.

Matthew 2:11-12, 16

Your visit to someone's house is a sign of your respect for him. The failure of the wise men to pass by the king Herod's court was a sign that they dishonoured him. The wise men simply did not show up at the palace of Herod. Their absence was a loud rebuke of disrespect towards the king. Herod himself realised that he had been despised.

3. Disregarding advice can be a sign of dishonour

Honour thy father and thy mother, as the Lord thy God hath commanded thee; that thy days may be prolonged, and that it may go well with thee, in the land which the Lord thy God giveth thee.

Deuteronomy 5:16

I once advised some church members not to go into debt. Although they sat there humbly and listened to all my preaching, they actually did not respect my words nor me. They completely disregarded my advice and some people actually entered into deep debt the very next week. The financial steps that they took showed complete disregard for me and my input.

To honour someone is to take notice of his advice and to try to follow it. Your attempting to follow his advice shows that you actually respect him. Those church members dishonoured me when they disregarded my advice. Indeed, some of them in their private moments said things like: "He doesn't know anything about living in America. What does he know about business? Things do not work without loans. He is a pastor, he doesn't know anything about financial engineering, leveraging, amortization, derivatives and mortgages".

My father once said to me, "Do not drive someone else's car". I have followed this advice although I could have disregarded it as being the ideas of an old man.

Disregarding someone's advice and input is a sign of dishonour. There are many governments that simply humour ministers of God. They completely disregard advice, counsel and inputs made by men of God. The advice they actually respect is the advice that is politically right. Anything that helps win an election and remain popular is considered good advice. The disregard of any advice coming from the church is a sign that they actually do not respect the church.

To dishonour someone is to disregard, ignore and to neglect the person's wisdom, thoughts, revelations, ideas and plans. When you ignore someone's teachings, you dishonour him, especially if you are part of a family that claims to be following him. Those who earnestly take note of your teachings and advice are those who honour you.

4. Leaving home can be a sign of dishonour

And when he came to himself, he said, How many hired servants of my father's have bread enough and to spare, and I perish with hunger!

I will arise and go to my father, and will say unto him, Father, I HAVE SINNED against heaven, and before thee,

Luke 15:17-18

The prodigal son dishonoured his father greatly by leaving home and not serving in the house. The sin that the prodigal son committed was the sin of not listening, not obeying, not deferring to his father. The elder son, on the other hand, honoured his father. He said, "All these years do I serve thee." In other words, "All these years I have been subject to you, I have deferred to you, I have obeyed you and I have submitted myself to you." The elder son honoured his father whilst the younger son dishonoured him.

When you leave home unceremoniously, you dishonour your parents. When you abandon the ministry, it is a sign that you dishonour it. When you walk away from your God-given position, it is a sign that you do not value or respect it any more. Your dishonour is seen when you leave and when you despise what you have known for many years. When you sneer at your father and walk away from the lifetime teaching and provision of your father, you are dishonouring him. This is exactly what the prodigal son did. It was not well with the prodigal son. It did

63

not turn out well at all for him. He lost all! He became poor. He became the last and the least.

Many pastors cannot rise and flourish because they dishonoured the house that trained them and raised them up. *Ministers who leave their houses are like dwarfs who cannot grow tall! Nothing that they do works. Prodigal sons do not prosper!* The prodigal son in the Bible did not prosper and the prodigal sons in the world today equally cannot prosper. It simply does not go well with them. The prophecy of Deuteronomy 5:16 is fulfilled in their lives over and over again.

> "Honour thy father and thy mother, as the LORD thy God hath commanded thee; that thy days may be prolonged, and THAT IT MAY GO WELL WITH THEE, in the land which the LORD thy God giveth thee"
>
> Deuteronomy 5:16

5. Your stubbornness can be a sign of your dishonour

> And the Lord spake unto Moses, saying, Speak unto the children of Israel, that they turn and encamp before Pi-hahiroth, between Migdol and the sea, over against Baal-zephon: before it shall ye encamp by the sea.
>
> For Pharaoh will say of the children of Israel, They are entangled in the land, the wilderness hath shut them in. And I will harden Pharaoh's heart, that he shall follow after them; and I WILL BE HONOURED UPON PHARAOH, AND UPON ALL HIS HOST; THAT THE EGYPTIANS MAY KNOW THAT I AM THE LORD. AND THEY DID SO.
>
> Exodus 14:1-4

> And the Lord said unto Moses, Wherefore criest thou unto me? Speak unto the children of Israel, that they go forward:
> But lift thou up thy rod, and stretch out thine hand over the sea, and divide it: and the children of Israel shall go on dry ground through the midst of the sea.

And I, behold, I will harden the hearts of the Egyptians, and they shall follow them: AND I WILL GET ME HONOUR UPON PHARAOH, AND UPON ALL HIS HOST, upon his chariots, and upon his horsemen.

And the Egyptians shall know that I am the Lord, when I have gotten me honour upon Pharaoh, upon his chariots, and upon his horsemen.

Exodus 14:15-18

God decided that He was going to be respected by Pharaoh. He was going to get Pharaoh to respect him. Pharaoh did not respect the God of the Hebrews. Jehovah decided to teach Pharaoh a lesson.

You are stubborn when it takes a long time for you to see and understand simple things. Pharaoh is an ultimate example of a stubborn person. He resisted God's instructions that came through the prophet Moses. Pharaoh did not respect the God of the Hebrews. He resisted the God of Israel. His stubbornness was a profound revelation of his disrespect for God.

Stubbornness reveals resistance. *When you are resistant towards somebody, you do not honour the person.* Your yieldedness and your flow reveal your honour! Answering back, arguing back reveal your dishonour and your resistance to instructions and ideas.

Silent refusal to obey and comply are also signs of dishonour. Fighting with a robber who is trying to have sex with you reveals your utter rejection of a despicable person. Your yieldedness and your flow towards your husband who is trying to have sex with you reveals the honour and recognition for him. Indeed, fighting back and resisting someone reveals your rejection and your lack of respect and acknowledgment for someone.

You dishonour me when you are stubborn towards me. Disobedience is manifested as stubbornness, resistance and rejection of authority. Pharaoh is the quintessential example of a stubborn person who dishonoured God's prophet. God's aim was to get His respect and honour out of Pharaoh.

6. Pretence and deception can be a sign of dishonour

Ye HYPOCRITES, well did Esaias prophesy of you, saying, This people draweth nigh unto me with their mouth, and HONOURETH ME WITH THEIR LIPS; but their heart is far from me. But in vain they do worship me, teaching for doctrines the commandments of men.

Matthew 15:7-9

Being a hypocrite, and pretending all the time is a sign that you think you can deceive someone. You esteem the person to have a lower intelligence. You think you can deceive him because you consider him to be a dimwit. When you try to humour or patronize an important person by saying things you don't believe, you may draw upon yourself the severest of rebukes. God did not take it lightly when His people feigned respect and pretended to honour Him when in fact their hearts were far from Him.

Over the years I have seen how people try to pretend towards me, telling me things they think I want to hear. When they are not with me they talk about everything else but when they are with me they talk about God and the church, they tell me their dreams and their desire to do missionary work.

They speak with a soft and gentle voice when they are speaking to me but they have a rough voice when they speak to others. Some even develop a special respectful accent when they are talking to me.

To honour someone is to be genuine and without pretence. Do not insult great people by assuming they are so in need of flattery, adulation and idolization. Do not insult great people by pretending around them. Do not assume they are so stupid to be taken in by your little act of false and pretentious humility.

66

CHAPTER 10

Stages of Dishonour

He is despised and rejected of men; a man of sorrows, and acquainted with grief:

and we hid as it were our faces from him; he was despised, and we esteemed him not.

Isaiah 53:3

The stages of dishonour can be studied by looking at the ministry of Jesus Christ. Jesus was progressively dishonoured until He was demeaned, disgraced, humiliated, despised and crucified like a mere criminal. The scripture above shows us what happened to Jesus Christ. How did things get so bad? Why did human beings treat Jesus Christ so dishonourably? Indeed, the people who lived in Jesus' times moved through all the stages of dishonour.

1. The first stage of dishonour is to be silent when you ought to speak.

> Is it lawful for us to give tribute unto Caesar, or no? But he perceived their craftiness, and said unto them, Why tempt ye me? Shew me a penny.
> Whose image and superscription hath it? They answered and said, Caesar's.
> And he said unto them, Render therefore unto Caesar the things which be Caesar's, and unto God the things which be God's.
> And they could not take hold of his words before the people: and THEY MARVELLED AT HIS ANSWER, AND HELD THEIR PEACE.
>
> Luke 20:22-26

The silence of the Pharisees was not out of respect for Jesus Christ and His doctrine. They did not respect Him. They were craftily tempting Him and trying to destroy Him.

Silence can be the beginning of disrespect and dishonour! Poor or zero communication can be a sign of someone dishonouring you!

When you are supposed to speak up and declare your stance, your silence can mean dishonour. When you make no comment, it may be a mild but real way of demonstrating dishonour. Your silence at certain times is a sign of your lack of faith, lack of respect and lack of support in what is going on.

Silence is a way to show disrespect. Jesus Christ did not honour Pilate's court by answering his questions. Jesus showed no respect to Pilate and his sham, unjust court by being silent. Jesus had no fear and no respect for Pilate.

"The Jews answered him, we have a law, and by our law he ought to die, because he made himself the Son of God. When Pilate therefore heard that saying, he was the more afraid; And went again into the judgment hall, and saith unto Jesus, Whence art thou? But Jesus gave him no answer. then saith Pilate unto him, speakest thou not unto me? knowest thou not that I have power to crucify thee, and have power to release thee? Jesus answered, Thou couldest have no power at all against me, except it were given thee from above: therefore he that delivered me unto thee hath the greater sin" (John 19:7-11).

There are times I have expected people to speak up in support of me. We have all had this experience. Some people think they can wisely hide behind diplomatic answers or silence. However, silence can have a devastating effect on the person who is expecting support. Silence can be the greatest message of disregard, disrespect and dishonour. Make sure you speak up when it is time to speak or you may lose your best friends!

2.   The second stage of dishonour is to not believe in someone.

After these things Jesus walked in Galilee: for he would not walk in Jewry, because the Jews sought to kill him. Now the Jews' feast of tabernacles was at hand.

His brethren therefore said unto him, Depart hence, and go into Judaea, that thy disciples also may see the works that thou doest.

For there is no man that doeth any thing in secret, and he himself seeketh to be known openly.

If thou do these things, shew thyself to the world. FOR NEITHER DID HIS BRETHREN BELIEVE IN HIM.

John 7:1-5

Jesus Christ experienced this stage of dishonour. There were many people who did not believe in Him. When you do not believe what someone says, it is a sign that you do not respect the person. A lack of faith is a lack of trust. In other words, you are saying, "You are not trustworthy. Your words are not worth much." Jesus' brothers did not believe in him.

Over the years, I have invited people to come into full-time ministry. Many of the people simply did not believe that it would be well with them. Their lack of belief was actually a lack of respect for full-time ministry and for the call of God. The same people have been ready to sacrifice everything and even live apart from their family for many years. Such people are ready to work donkey hours for various secular causes. They simply have no faith in full-time ministry. They had no faith and respect for the call of God. They had no respect for my offer to work for the Lord. Not believing and not obeying are sure signs of a lack of honour.

3. The third stage of dishonour is to reject someone.

And it came to pass, when the time was come that he should be received up, he stedfastly set his face to go to Jerusalem, And sent messengers before his face: and they went, and entered into a village of the Samaritans, to make ready for him. AND THEY DID NOT RECEIVE HIM, BECAUSE HIS FACE WAS AS THOUGH HE WOULD GO TO JERUSALEM.

Luke 9:51-53

And they that fed the swine fled, and told it in the city, and in the country. And they went out to see what it was that was done.

And they come to Jesus, and see him that was possessed with the devil, and had the legion, sitting, and clothed, and in his right mind: and they were afraid. And they that saw it told them how it befell to him that was possessed with the devil, and also concerning the swine.

AND THEY BEGAN TO PRAY HIM TO DEPART OUT OF THEIR COASTS. And when he was come into the ship, he that had been possessed with the devil prayed him that he might be with him. Howbeit Jesus suffered him not, but saith unto him, Go home to thy friends, and tell them how great things the Lord hath done for thee, and hath had compassion on thee.

Mark 5:14-19

Jesus experienced every stage of dishonour! The next stage of dishonour is open rejection. This is a more advanced form of dishonour.

Rejection is to be asked to leave! It is to be asked to get out! It is to be asked not to come near! Jesus Christ was rejected by a village of Samaritans. He was also rejected in the country of the Gadarenes. When you are asked to leave it is a great sign of dishonour. On occasion, you may be openly rejected by people who do not regard you at all. There are times we have attempted to have crusades in certain cities where the pastors have refused to host us.

We have experienced hostility and rejection from certain countries where we were told categorically that we were not welcome. When you are rejected, it is because they do not respect you. If some other person was coming they may have opened their arms and doors to them. Watch out for those who reject you outright. It is a sign that they do not honour you. Those whom they honour, they receive!

4. The fourth stage of dishonour is to prevent others from honouring someone.

And being in Bethany in the house of Simon the leper, as he sat at meat, there came a woman having an alabaster box of ointment of spikenard very precious; and she brake the box, and poured it on his head.

And THERE WERE SOME THAT HAD INDIGNATION WITHIN THEMSELVES, AND SAID, WHY WAS THIS WASTE OF THE OINTMENT MADE?

For it might have been sold for more than three hundred pence, and have been given to the poor. And they murmured against her. AND JESUS SAID, LET HER ALONE; WHY TROUBLE YE HER? She hath wrought a good work on me.

Mark 14:3-6

Jesus also experienced this stage of dishonour. The next stage of dishonour is to prevent others from honouring you. Jesus was being honoured by the woman with the alabaster box. However, some disciples were against the idea. "It's too much" they said. It is too expensive. It is not necessary. That is a waste of money! Who is he? Is he God? Why all this fuss about one man? Some people are simply against the honouring of God's servant. If you want to give an offering to God's servant, they would always suggest a lower amount. Don't give too much! Don't spoil him! It is too much! This is not a bank! He just preached for forty minutes.

Indeed, there are always people who sit at meetings and dissuade others from honouring you. I was once at a meeting where suggestions were made for ministers to be speakers at a programme. When certain names were mentioned, the suggestions were immediately shot down by others.

Someone said, "He shouts too much." Another said, "We don't want his brand of charismatism." Another said, "There are questions about this man so let's stay off any controversy." Another said, "We wouldn't want his name associated with this programme."

In a few moments, honoured servants of God were set-aside as though they were lepers. Indeed, there are people who prevent others from being honoured. They fight against the lifting and honouring of others. Make sure you are not someone who fights against the honouring of God's servants.

5. **The fifth stage of dishonour is to accuse, to quarrel and to be in conflict with someone.**

And the whole multitude of them arose, and led him unto Pilate. AND THEY BEGAN TO ACCUSE HIM, SAYING, we found this fellow perverting the nation, and forbidding to give tribute to Caesar, saying that he himself is Christ a King.

Luke 23:1-2

Jesus Christ experienced this fifth stage of dishonour. When you accuse someone, you dishonour the person. It is demeaning for someone to be accused of evil and wrongdoing. When you go to court, the accused person is the least respected person in the court. He is virtually a criminal until proven otherwise. The judge is respected! The lawyers are respected! The senior lawyers are respected even more! But the accused person is the villain of the courtroom. He may not have done what he is accused of but he is still disregarded and dishonoured.

Be careful of accusations. Accusations lower the person who is accused. They degrade him and reduce him and his character. Jesus Christ was reduced to a mere criminal.

You must be aware that your accusations of someone represent the dishonour you have for him. The opposition party disrespects and disregards the plans and purposes of the ruling party so they criticise and accuse the ruling party all the time. Criticism and accusations are clear signs of dishonour.

6. **The sixth stage of dishonour is to physically attack a person.**

Then the soldiers of the governor took Jesus into the common hall, and gathered unto him the whole band of soldiers. And they stripped him, and put on him a scarlet robe. And when they had platted a crown of thorns, they put it upon his head, and a reed in his right hand: and they bowed the knee before him, and mocked him, saying, Hail, King of the Jews!

And they spit upon him, and took the reed, and smote him on the head. And after that they had mocked him, they took the robe off from him, and put his own raiment on him, and led him away to crucify him. And as they came out, they found a man of Cyrene, Simon by name: him they compelled to bear his cross.

And when they were come unto a place called Golgotha, that is to say, a place of a skull, They gave him vinegar to drink mingled with gall: and when he had tasted thereof, he would not drink. And they crucified him, and parted his garments, casting lots: that it might be fulfilled which was spoken by the prophet, they parted my garments among them, and upon my vesture did they cast lots.

And sitting down they watched him there; And set up over his head his accusation written, THIS IS JESUS THE KING OF THE JEWS. Then were there two thieves crucified with him, one on the right hand, and another on the left. And they that passed by reviled him, wagging their heads, And saying, Thou that destroyest the temple, and buildest it in three days, save thyself. If thou be the Son of God, come down from the cross. Likewise also the chief priests mocking him, with the scribes and elders, said, He saved others; himself he cannot save. If he be the King of Israel, let him now come down from the cross, and we will believe him.

Matthew 27:27-42

The last stage of dishonour is to physically attack a person. This is what happened to Jesus Christ. Jesus Christ was dishonoured throughout His ministry on earth. He came to His own and His own received Him not. He was dishonoured constantly by the Pharisees and others who hated His honest, truthful preaching.

Finally, Jesus Christ was openly attacked and dishonoured by the soldiers of the Roman Empire. The Pharisees and their militia men openly assaulted Jesus Christ and whipped Him. Whenever God's servant is openly attacked, we have reached the highest level of dishonour.

All that happened to Jesus on the cross was a culmination of what had happened to Him in the past three years that He ministered. He had been dishonoured in many different ways.

One day, after preaching at a programme, I felt that the church did not appreciate my preaching and my efforts to minister to them. I did not feel honoured by the church or by its pastor. I had various signs to prove that I was not honoured there.

But I was to receive even greater dishonour. When I received a threat that I would be attacked for my preaching, I knew that the dishonour from that encounter was real. Anytime a physical attack is threatened, you no longer need evidence that you are dishonoured. You do not have to read any more signs.

When dishonour is in the form of silence, disbelief, rejection and accusations, you may not be sure of what is happening to you. But when an open attack is threatened, you can be sure that you have encountered the highest level of dishonour.

CHAPTER 11

The Results of Dishonour

Jesus answered, I HAVE NOT A DEVIL; BUT I HONOUR MY FATHER, and ye do dishonour me. And I seek not mine own glory: there is one that seeketh and judgeth.

John 8:49-50

1. Dishonour results in a demonic invasion of your life.

Jesus answered, I HAVE NOT A DEVIL; BUT I HONOUR
MY FATHER, and ye do dishonour me. And I seek not
mine own glory: there is one that seeketh and judgeth.

John 8:49-50

Jesus said He did not have a devil! Jesus was sure that He did
not have a devil because He honoured His father. If you do
not honour your father you cannot be sure that you do not have
a devil. Indeed, people who dishonour their parents have devils
working in their lives. You can be sure you do not have a devil
when you honour your father.

The demons that cause struggles, hassles and frustrations are
the portion of those who dishonour their fathers. When Vashti
dishonoured her husband, the devils of demotion invaded her life.

Then entered Satan into Judas surnamed Iscariot, being of
the number of the twelve.

Luke 22:3

Judas dishonoured Jesus by betraying Him. Judas dishonoured
Jesus by even thinking about betraying Jesus. Judas received
the devil into his soul when he dishonoured the appointment that
Jesus gave him as an apostle. When you dishonour God's calling
and appointment, demons will invade your life.

They sacrificed unto devils, not to God; to gods whom
they knew not, to new gods that came newly up, whom
your fathers feared not.

Deuteronomy 32:17

Those who fail to honour God's calling usually end up with
demons in their homes and lives. You either sacrifice to God or
to devils. When you sacrifice to God, it is because you honour
Him. When you do not sacrifice to God and honour God, you
end up with devils.

2. Dishonour results in you entering obscure darkness.

> Whoso curseth his father or his mother, his lamp shall be
> put out in obscure darkness.
>
> Proverbs 20:20

When you curse your father, you go into darkness. When you dishonour your father, you move into obscurity. You will be enveloped in darkness and obscurity when you dishonour those who raised you.

This is why pastors who break away from their spiritual homes rarely flourish. The scripture says they will be in obscurity. To be in obscurity means you will be unimportant and insignificant. Many pastors who fight their fathers are no longer important in ministry. Their churches are insignificant and their voices are no longer heard.

You are cursed with obscurity, insignificance and unimportance when you dishonour your father: Your lamp will not go out in normal darkness but in obscure darkness.

Darkness is a symbol of difficulty. You will be forced to live in difficulty because you dishonour those who brought you up.

Your lamp will go out! This curse is reserved for dishonourable sons and daughters. This means you will be extinguished, you will disappear and you will be found no more.

3. Dishonour results in you being replaced.

> What shall we do unto the queen Vashti according to law, because she hath not performed the commandment of the king Ahasuerus by the chamberlains? And Memucan answered before the king and the princes, Vashti the queen hath not done wrong to the king only, but also to all the princes, and to all the people that are in all the provinces of the king Ahasuerus.
>
> For this deed of the queen shall come abroad unto all women, so that they shall despise their husbands in their

eyes, when it shall be reported, The king Ahasuerus commanded Vashti the queen to be brought in before him, but she came not. Likewise shall the ladies of Persia and Media say this day unto all the king's princes, which have heard of the deed of the queen. Thus shall there arise too much contempt and wrath.

If it please the king, let there go a royal commandment from him, and let it be written among the laws of the Persians and the Medes, that it be not altered, that Vashti come no more before king Ahasuerus; and let the king give her royal estate unto another that is better than she. And when the king's decree which he shall make shall be published throughout all his empire, (for it is great,) ALL THE WIVES SHALL GIVE TO THEIR HUSBANDS HONOUR, BOTH TO GREAT AND SMALL.

Esther 1:15-20

Vashti did not give honour to her husband. She lost her position. She was replaced by a more humble person. The reward for dishonour is to lose your place.

You lose respect and honour when you dishonour those you must honour. You will no longer be celebrated. Vashti was no longer celebrated. Vashti was no longer invited! Vashti was no longer wanted! Vashti was no longer honoured! This is what happens to those who fail to honour what God says they should honour. Vashti failed to honour her husband and she lost the honour of being the wife of the King.

4. Dishonour results in you being lightly esteemed.

Wherefore the LORD God of Israel saith, I said indeed that thy house, and the house of thy father, should walk before me for ever: but now the LORD saith, Be it far from me; for them that honour me I will honour, and THEY THAT DESPISE ME SHALL BE LIGHTLY ESTEEMED.

1 Samuel 2:30

The reward for not honouring God was to lose all honour and to be lightly esteemed. Beware of dishonour! It is your seed for future dishonour and being lightly esteemed by others.

Many people dishonour God when they take His calling lightly. They prefer to work for unbelievers than to work for Jesus. They prefer to go for missions for the United Nations or the UNHCR, the WHO or the Red Cross. They are prepared to be in any country of the world for any of these organisations. Many people are happy that their children work for such organisations, even if it is in the most dangerous countries of the world. But they despise and reject the idea that their children would be missionaries to the nations of the world. Remember that as you despise God, He will also lightly esteem you!

Perhaps you wonder why you are lightly esteemed in this life. People have been surprised at the respect that men of God receive in the world. Who are they? Why should they be honoured? Why should they be respected? Why should any one take notice of them? It is because you have lightly esteemed God's work and God's house. You allowed your child to go to medical school but you did not allow your child to go to the bible school. You allowed your child to go on a UN mission but you did not allow your child to go on a soul winning mission! Over the years, I have seen people demean full-time ministry. I have watched as people have disregarded the job of ministry and priesthood. They would not come into full-time ministry and they would not want anyone they knew to come into full-time ministry either.

I have had wives warn their husbands to stay away from me so that they would not be contaminated with the idea of working in full-time ministry. Is that not the demeaning of full-time ministry? Why wouldn't you want your husband to work for the Lord? Is it not an honourable thing to work for the Lord? Who should be in full-time ministry? Should it be only idiots and ne'er do wells that work for God?

I have had families send their drug addicted children to the bible school to become pastors when they were still hooked onto their drugs. I have had people send their children with schizophrenia and other mental illnesses to the bible school. I have had people sending their children with hydrocephalus and severe mental retardation to the bible school. These same people would not send their normal children to the bible school to become pastors. They send their normal children to the university and their abnormal, uncontrollable children to the bible school. They assume that God's work should be done by social dropouts and mentally ill people. This is the highest kind of dishonour to the work of ministry. It is an insult to the intelligence of God. Watch out for those who dishonour the work of ministry.

Perhaps some of the most blatant examples of dishonour have come from spouses whose husbands or wives are in full-time ministry. I have seen husbands show disregard for their wives who are in full-time ministry. They give instructions to their wives as though their wife's work is a useless waste of time. They fight, oppose, demean and degrade the job their wives do constantly from behind the scenes. They oppose their working hours, their travels and insult their bosses from the comfort of their homes.

It is amazing that such people also go to church and want to have a church with a pastor. However, they do not want their families to ever work in the church because they have the spirit of Eli's sons who demean the work of the priest. Be careful of the disrespect you show to the office of ministry!

Remember that as you do not honour God and His servants, God will also lightly esteem you! Perhaps you wonder why you are so lightly esteemed in this life!

5. Dishonour results in you not seeing the power of God.

And when the sabbath day was come, he began to teach in the synagogue: and many hearing him were astonished, saying, From whence hath this man these things? And what wisdom is this which is given unto him, that even such mighty works are wrought by his hands?

Is not this the carpenter, the son of Mary, the brother of James, and Joses, and of Juda, and Simon? And are not his sisters here with us? And they were offended at him. But Jesus said unto them, a prophet is not without honour, but in his own country, and among his own kin, and in his own house.

And HE COULD THERE DO NO MIGHTY WORK, save that he laid his hands upon a few sick folk, and healed them.

Mark 6:2-5

Almighty God refused to do mighty works and miracles in Nazareth. His great power was withheld in this city where He was dishonoured. Your dishonour and disrespect for Jesus will ensure that you never see great power, signs and wonders in your life and ministry.

CHAPTER 12

Move Away From Those Who Dishonour You

And he could there do no mighty work, save that he laid his hands upon a few sick folk, and healed them. And he marvelled because of their unbelief. And he went round about the villages, teaching.

Mark 6:5-6

The sixth chapter of Mark contains the story of how Jesus was dishonoured in His hometown. But it also contains the story of how Jesus moved away from the place of dishonour and began to experience the amazing power of God. The life and ministry of Jesus are the best guide for your ministry! If it happened to Jesus, you can only expect that it will happen to you. If Jesus overcame His problems in a particular way, you must expect to overcome your problems in the same way.

Jesus moved away from the people who dishonoured Him. He did not stay to explain to them how He was the Son of God and how He had many blessings in store for them. People who reject you must equally be abandoned. You must find those who believe in you, who believe in your calling. You must move away from those who dishonour you because Jesus moved away from those who dishonoured Him.

In the beginning of the sixth chapter of Mark's gospel, Jesus was greatly dishonoured in Nazareth. As you read on in the sixth chapter of Mark you see Jesus moving away from Nazareth into places where the power of God could work. As Jesus moved further and further away from Nazareth, the anointing began to work and the power began to flow. Financial miracles took place as Jesus commissioned disciples to go out on missions, even without money.

Jesus Moved Away from Areas of Dishonour

And he said unto them, COME YE YOURSELVES APART INTO A DESERT PLACE, and rest a while: for there were many coming and going, and they had no leisure so much as to eat. And they departed into a desert place by ship privately. And when they had passed over, they came into the land of Gennesaret, and drew to the shore.

Mark 6:31-32, 53

And when they had passed over, THEY CAME INTO THE LAND OF GENNESARET, and drew to the shore. And when they were come out of the ship, straightway they knew him, and ran through that whole region round about, and began to carry about in beds those that were sick, where they heard he was. And whithersoever he entered, into villages, or cities, or country, they laid the sick in the streets, and besought him that they might touch if it were but the border of his garment: and as many as touched him were made whole.

Mark 6:53-56

1. Move away from dishonour and experience miracles of provision.

Great miracles of provision are not possible where the ministry is not honoured. Where a man of God is not honoured, there is little financial breakthrough. I have missionaries and pastors who are honoured in their churches. They experience many financial blessings. Those pastors who are not honoured in their churches do not experience financial breakthrough and are always in difficulty.

And he marvelled because of their unbelief. And he went round about the villages, teaching.

And he called unto him the twelve, and began to send them forth by two and two; and gave them power over unclean spirits; And commanded them that they should take nothing for their journey, save a staff only; no scrip, no bread, no money in their purse: But be shod with sandals; and not put on two coats.

And he said unto them, in what place soever ye enter into an house, there abide till ye depart from that place.

Mark 6:6-10

2. Move away from dishonour and experience the power to send anointed people on missions.

And he called unto him the twelve, and began to send them forth by two and two; and gave them power over unclean spirits;

Mark 6:7

And they cast out many devils, and anointed with oil many that were sick, and healed them. And king Herod heard of him; (for his name was spread abroad:) and he said, That John the Baptist was risen from the dead, and therefore mighty works do shew forth themselves in him. Others said, that it is Elias. And others said, that it is a prophet, or as one of the prophets.

Mark 6:13-15

3. Move away from dishonour and experience great financial miracles of provision.

The famous miracle of the loaves and fishes happened in the sixth chapter of Mark, shortly after Jesus was despised in Nazareth. What an amazing miracle of provision; feeding five thousand people! Most of us can hardly feed our households. But Jesus had such miracle power working in His life and ministry, that thousands were fed and sustained. You will also have supernatural power to sustain and to feed thousands of people when you move away from those who despise you. Do not struggle to prove yourself to people! Just move on and you will experience great provision and great power.

And when the day was now far spent, his disciples came unto him, and said, This is a desert place, and now the time is far passed: Send them away, that they may go into the country round about, and into the villages, and buy themselves bread: for they have nothing to eat. He answered and said unto them, Give ye them to eat. And they say unto him, Shall we go and buy two hundred pennyworth of bread, and give them to eat?

He saith unto them, how many loaves have ye? Go and see. And when they knew, they say, five, and two fishes. And he commanded them to make all sit down by companies upon the green grass. And they sat down in ranks, by hundreds, and by fifties. AND WHEN HE HAD TAKEN THE FIVE LOAVES AND THE TWO FISHES, HE LOOKED UP TO HEAVEN, AND BLESSED, AND BRAKE THE LOAVES, AND GAVE THEM TO HIS

DISCIPLES TO SET BEFORE THEM; AND THE TWO FISHES DIVIDED HE AMONG THEM ALL. AND THEY DID ALL EAT, AND WERE FILLED. And they took up twelve baskets full of the fragments, and of the fishes.

Mark 6:35-43

4. Move away from dishonour and experience signs and wonders in your ministry.

Jesus went on to walk on water when He left His hometown. In His hometown, He did not perform any amazing feats. Walking on water is one of the greatest demonstrations of miracle power ever known to man. Walking on water is almost as significant as raising the dead. It is simply something that is impossible to human beings. All these fantastic displays of power were not possible when Jesus was dishonoured in His hometown. Do not expect to experience the power of God where you are dishonoured. It is where people respect you that you will see the greatness of your ministry. That is where you will see the dew of heaven and the fatness of the earth.

And when he had sent them away, he departed into a mountain to pray. And when even was come, the ship was in the midst of the sea, and he alone on the land. And he saw them toiling in rowing; for the wind was contrary unto them: and ABOUT THE FOURTH WATCH OF THE NIGHT HE COMETH UNTO THEM, WALKING UPON THE SEA, and would have passed by them.

But when they saw him walking upon the sea, they supposed it had been a spirit, and cried out: For they all saw him, and were troubled. And immediately he talked with them, and saith unto them, be of good cheer: it is I; be not afraid.

And he went up unto them into the ship; and the wind ceased: and they were sore amazed in themselves beyond measure, and wondered.

Mark 6:46-51

5. Move away from dishonour and experience awesome power and great miracles of healing.

The whole region heard of Jesus and began to carry sick people on their beds to seek Jesus. Imagine the sick being lined up on the streets so that your shadow or the border of your garment would touch them. What awesome power was available in the sixth chapter of Mark! Yet, in the very first verse of Mark 6, Jesus was unable to operate in the healing ministry. He had to lay hands on people. And even then just a few minor miracles were performed. Amazing displays of miraculous power of healing took place even without any prayer or laying on of hands. All these were not possible when Jesus was in His hometown. Thank God for the wisdom of moving away from the place where you are dishonoured!

> And when they had passed over, they came into the land of Gennesaret, and drew to the shore. And when they were come out of the ship, straightway they knew him, and ran through that whole region round about, and began to carry about in beds those that were sick, where they heard he was.
>
> And whithersoever he entered, into villages, or cities, or country, THEY LAID THE SICK IN THE STREETS, AND BESOUGHT HIM THAT THEY MIGHT TOUCH IF IT WERE BUT THE BORDER OF HIS GARMENT: AND AS MANY AS TOUCHED HIM WERE MADE WHOLE.
>
> Mark 6:53-56

CHAPTER 13

Honouring with Ease

Render therefore to all their dues: tribute to whom tribute is due; custom to whom custom; fear to whom fear; honour to whom honour.

Romans 13:7

Do not let the concept of honouring be a problem for you any more. You are not a rebel! You are not a disloyal person! You are not a dishonourable child! You are walking in the glory of God! You are doing the will of God! The Holy Spirit is guiding you! You will render to everyone their dues. You will give honour to whom honour is due!

1. Honour with love and faith.

Some people struggle with the concept of honouring another human being. It is time for you to believe in the beauty and the blessings of honouring those to whom it is due. If you truly understand what it is, you will begin to enjoy honouring those who deserve the honour.

Mary and Martha loved Jesus Christ. That is why they honoured Him effortlessly.

If you love someone, you will honour the person. Honour and respect are natural products of love. When a person is loved, he is honoured!

It is important that you tune all your relationships to the love frequency. You must love your husband; then you will honour him naturally. You must love your pastor; then you will honour him naturally. It is when you do not love someone that honouring him becomes a problem.

Even in the secular world, children who dislike their parents are set aside. Because they dislike their parents they do not honour them. Sometimes, outsiders who love, honour and cherish the person are brought close and given amazing benefits. There are many stories of rich men whose children despised their fathers.

Many children of rich people are spoilt brats. They do not know why they have what they have. They do not know how fortunate they are. They do not understand the hard work of their parents that has given them all they have. It is often outsiders who are filled with admiration for the hardworking man. History is replete with stories of those who received blessings because they honoured.

I heard of a billionaire who gave 5 million dollars to his housekeeper and a hundred dollars to each of his children.

When I was in medical school, I heard of a rich man who gave millions of dollars to his cat. He said the cat should be looked after in a home and research should be done for cat illnesses. To his wife, he gave a Bible so that it would help her to change her rude and disrespectful ways.

I also heard of a maid who won a notorious legal battle with a family of six children for a three hundred million dollar estate. This maid had looked after her boss and her boss decided to give her his estate, instead of giving it to his ungrateful and disrespectful children.

Another story of honour was about Cara Wood. In 1992, Cara Wood was 17 and working at Drin's Colonial Restaurant in her hometown of Chagrin Falls, about 15 miles east of Cleveland. She was a good employee – bright, friendly and helpful. One customer, Bill Cruxton, liked her so much that he always sat in her section. A widower with no children, he went daily to the restaurant for his meals and some company, so they became friends. In addition to being his regular waitress, she helped him around the house and ran errands for him. Wood became so important to Cruxton that he rewrote his will, making her the main beneficiary. Cruxton, 82, died of heart failure in November 1992 and left her half a million dollars.

2. Honour with acceptance and admiration.

Mary and Martha accepted and admired Jesus Christ.

Without accepting the man of God, you cannot do much. You cannot receive from him and you will never feel like honouring him. You have to accept the person whom God has sent. This woman accepted that Jesus Christ was the Messiah. She believed that Jesus Christ was the great prophet. She believed that He was holy. She believed that He could forgive sins. She accepted Him. That is why she could honour Him!

Do you accept the people that God has brought into your life? Do you accept that they are great and wonderful prophets and pastors to you? Admiration is the key to honouring with ease!

Without admiration your mouth will not be open and your heart will not be turned towards your master. Mary saw Jesus as the greatest and the best. That is why she lay down at His feet and wept before Him. It was admiration that made her use her hair to wipe His feet. Her heart was completely open towards Jesus Christ.

Admiration is what causes honour to be easy for you to give.

3. Honour with a conviction.

Mary had a conviction that other bystanders did not have. You cannot force people to honour God's servant. You cannot force people to honour God. You have to have a belief and a conviction that will make you honour God or His servant.

I once had a dream that I was to honour a man of God. In the dream, the Lord spoke to me and told me that if I did not honour him I would not get to certain heights in ministry. Since then, I have tried to honour this man of God. I have had enough experiences, and perhaps reasons, not to honour him. It is my conviction that keeps me on the road of honouring the man of God. I honour him easily because I have the conviction to do so.

Without a deep-seated conviction, you will never really be able to honour a man of God. You will always find a reason not to. For instance, you may find out that the man of God you want to honour is far wealthier than you are. Why should you give money to someone who does not need it? Why should you give money to someone who has far more than you have? These are good logical reasons to keep you away from honouring God's servant.

I once prepared an offering to give to a man of God. Just before I could see him to present my offering, he mentioned in his preaching that his tithes for that year had been something like twenty-five million dollars. I thought to myself, "Wow! Twenty-five million dollars! That means his income for that year was about two hundred and fifty million dollars." I thought to myself, "This man is super wealthy. I do not even have one million dollars. Why should I give him my crumbs?"

That was a good logical reason not to honour the man of God. But God spoke to me to honour him, even though he had far more than I did.

Obeying God in that was one of the best decisions of my life! Honouring that man of God was very important to my life and ministry. I was not meeting his financial needs. I just needed to honour him! That was the will of God!

4. Honour according to rank.

To flow in the grace of honouring people, you need to honour everyone according to their rank. It is much easier to honour people according to who they really are in your life. You cannot honour someone above the person's rank. You must not honour someone who is not as important with the same honour you give to a more important person.

And the child Samuel grew on, and was in favour both with the Lord, and also with men. And there came a man of God unto Eli, and said unto him, Thus saith the Lord, Did I plainly appear unto the house of thy father, when they were in Egypt in Pharaoh's house? And did I choose him out of all the tribes of Israel to be my priest, to offer upon mine altar, to burn incense, to wear an ephod before me? And did I give unto the house of thy father all the offerings made by fire of the children of Israel? Wherefore kick ye at my sacrifice and at mine offering, which I have commanded in my habitation; AND HONOUREST THY

SONS ABOVE ME, to make yourselves fat with the chiefest of all the offerings of Israel my people?

Wherefore the Lord God of Israel saith, I said indeed that thy house, and the house of thy father, should walk before me for ever: but now the Lord saith, Be it far from me; FOR THEM THAT HONOUR ME I WILL HONOUR, AND THEY THAT DESPISE ME SHALL BE LIGHTLY ESTEEMED.

1 Samuel 2:26-30

When Eli decided not to publicly denounce and dismiss his sons, he was actually honouring them. He was showing them respect. He was giving them some honour. Unfortunately, this respect that he granted his sons was a sign that he had not given God the honour that He could have. God did not take this lightly and released one of the most withering curses on Eli.

If someone advises you, you may choose to reject his advice. If another person advises you to do the same exact thing and you rather obey the second person, then you have honoured the second person more than the first.

For example, your husband may ask you to run up the staircase and you may disobey him. If your pastor tells you to run up the same staircase and you obey him, then your pastor is more honoured than your husband!

Indeed, in honouring your pastor's instruction, you have shown that you actually despise your husband's instruction.

If a man of God comes to preach in your church, you may give him a hundred dollars as an honorarium. Another man of God may also be a speaker at the same program. You may choose to give him only ten dollars as an honorarium. The honour you gave to the first person by giving him a hundred dollars shows that you honour him more. A hundred dollars is more substantial honour than ten dollars.

A founder and father of a church felt that he was not being honoured in his church. He felt that other visitors were honoured more than he was honoured in the very church he had founded. Indeed, the scripture teaches us to honour our fathers, not our uncles. You cannot honour your uncle more than you honour your father.

So he asked his resident pastor, "How much honorarium did you give to this preacher who came to your church." He found out that the visiting preacher was honoured far more than he the father and founder of the church. The church had taken their founder and senior pastor for granted and were honouring the visitors and uncles far more than the founder.

One day, a pastor conducted a convention in his church. At the end of the service, a man came up and presented a brand new Toyota Land Cruiser as a gift to the visiting prophet. The senior pastor was happy that the visiting prophet had received such a large gift. However, he was amazed that his church members would honour a visiting prophet so highly but had never seen the need to give him even a small Toyota car.

5. Honour with humility.

Humility is an important step in honouring someone. Without humility, you will not see the greatness of a person as you should. The anointing does not flow upwards. Anointing does not flow horizontally. If you are not humble in relation to a person, you cannot honour him.

Honour is upward. You do not honour somebody who is below you. Honour is usually directed at someone above you. Failure to honour is often evidence of pride.

The woman with the alabaster box is a great example of the beauty of a humble person who honours another. This lady humbled herself by kneeling down and even using her hair to wipe Jesus' feet. That is a very humble act. *It is because you are not small in your own eyes that certain ministers are not great to you.*

Mary was humble. She honoured Jesus greatly. She brought an alabaster box of oil and honoured Jesus famously. She is noted for the unusual honour she bestowed on Jesus, by pouring an expensive alabaster box of ointment on Him. Many people have the experience of having a very great man of God in their lives, in their homes or in their offices but few ever honour a man of God in this way.

Jesus did not rebuke this lady! Jesus did not warn her to stay away from Him. Jesus did not correct her, as He did with many other people. He rather said she was doing a good thing. She was memorialized and will be remembered far more than any man of God can ever hope for. Indeed, giving honour is an important act with far reaching consequences!

6. Honour before it is too late.

Mary honoured Jesus Christ in time. Most people are not quick to recognize greatness. The greatness of a person is often recognized after they die. Their absence and the effect of their absence are not easy to ignore. Whilst they are alive, they are often criticized or ignored. It is almost as though everyone is waiting for your death to say good things about you and to spend money on you. If you want to honour someone, it is important that you rush to do so now.

I remember when the Archbishop Idahosa came to Ghana. I felt convicted in my heart to honour him. I decided to find out which hotel he was staying in and present him with a special offering. I had a deep conviction in my heart that it was something I needed to do.

He was both touched and surprised by this gesture of mine. He laid hands on me and prayed for me in his hotel room. One morning two weeks later, after he had left Ghana, I got a call that the Archbishop Idahosa had just died. I could not believe my ears. When he prayed for me two weeks before, he had been hale and hearty. There was nothing wrong with him and there was no sign of death on him. As I pondered over my interaction with him two weeks earlier, I realised that God had urged me to honour him before it was too late.

REFERENCES

Chapter 13

1. *10 Unbelievable Inheritance Stories* Retrieved from https://www.oddee.com/item_96948.aspx May 2019